WHAT A TROUT SEES

A Fly-Fishing Guide to Life Underwater

GEOFF MUELLER

LYONS PRESS
Guilford, Connecticut
An imprint of Globe Pequot Press

To the rivers—those I know well, and those I've yet to meet

Lyons Press is an imprint of Globe Pequot Press.

Interior photos by Tim Romano unless otherwise noted.

Project Editor: David Legere
Text Design: Sue Murray
Layout Artist: Melissa Evarts

Library of Congress Cataloging-in-Publication Data is available on file.

ISBN 978-0-7627-7984-0

Printed in the United States of America
10 9 8 7 6 5 4 3 2 1

Contents

Foreword

The first group of fish I ever truly observed remained in my memory for years. They were summer steelhead, holed up on Oregon's Nestucca River, a coastal stream that gets pretty thin by midsummer as it flows some forty miles from the Coast Range to Tillamook Bay.

As an eleven year old with a fascination for steelhead, I stared at them for hours, sitting on a rock ledge over the river, wondering if a crawdad tail would do the trick. It never did, but my lack of success in catching them never took away from my joy of watching them fin around at the bottom of that pool.

Since then, I've snorkeled with saltwater species, spotted chinook from helicopters, and spent hours patiently waiting for carp to swim past me in my local pond. But this notion of what a trout sees, or what they watch and do when we *aren't* fishing for them, took on a whole new meaning this past fall, when I learned what watching fish was really all about.

Lee Spencer has been the guardian of steelhead on the North Umpqua's Steamboat Creek for fourteen years, spending six months a season just *watching* the fish and protecting spawning adults from poachers. The vast knowledge this man possesses from years on his post is testimony to just how much a person can learn by truly observing and discovering. Spencer understands—as Geoff Mueller and Tim Romano have come to understand—that your senses get more acute as you gain focus on the fish.

Lee Spencer's deep knowledge comes primarily from watching from above the water, focusing on one particular group of extraordinary fish. Mueller takes a broader brush to the concept in this book, by focusing above and below the water, and by passing what he learns onto fellow anglers.

Mueller and Romano are two of the sharpest young minds in fly fishing today. Both are actively engaged in many aspects of the sport—Geoff as senior editor of *The Drake* magazine and a frequent contributor to *Angling Trade,* and Tim as a photographer, co-publisher of *AT,* and a founder of the Greenbacks—a Trout Unlimited subgroup of young fly fishers. This book says much about the value of stopping and looking at rising fish before wading into a stream. What are they *doing?* Are they agitated? Calm? Aggressive? Timid? Eating emergers? Adults? Is it a spinner fall?

Mueller brings a thoughtful, curious approach to his writing, something that was honed during his time as a newspaper reporter. He researches more than most, and he loves the history of the sport, which adds much to the finished product.

While he's a great fisherman, I believe even more important is Mueller's passion for the sport itself. He *loves* to fish. This was a bit of a concern to me when I hired him nearly three years ago. Did I really want, as my first real employee, someone who loves to fish as much as I do? Is this a good thing or a bad thing? Will he even show up for work in the summertime? I'd had some experience with this issue as editor of *Powder* magazine, when I would get the 9 a.m. phone call from a junior editor asking if it was cool to extend his assignment for a couple days as they were "snowed in" and couldn't get out. Or sometimes it was the e-mail request for one more day of heliskiing—with one foot already in the chopper.

My concerns proved mostly unwarranted with Mueller (as long as salmonflies weren't hatching on the Poudre [or the North Platte] [or the Encampment]). He proved to me that being a consistently good writer and editor means not only having a handle on style and grammar (Mueller speaks Canadian, but has a good grasp on English anyway), but also a strong passion for the subject matter. He can tell a fishing story without it sounding like a fishing story, and he has an ability to find the characters that drive a good narrative. He can also consistently catch larger smallmouth than me, and he even, somehow, learned to row.

He's still a quirky Canadian, but lucky for me, his eye for good writing and good photos is better than his eye for a good shirt. If you need to borrow a funky flannel from '91, he's your man, and if you're looking to learn something new about this sport that we all love—or at least look at a familiar scene from a different perspective—then I believe you'll enjoy this book. After all, there is a time to be the hard-charging, take-no-prisoners agro angler. But there is also a time for patience and keen observation—both above and below the surface. May this book help you find knowledge and success and a deeper understanding of trout.

Tom Bie

Tom Bie is the editor and publisher of *The Drake* magazine, a quarterly fly-fishing publication that he founded in 1998. He formerly worked for the *Jackson Hole Guide* newspaper, and *Paddler, Skiing,* and *Powder* magazines, as well as being a fly-fishing guide in Jackson from 1993–1999. He is a 1991 journalism graduate of Oregon State University and is also a veteran of the US Army. Bie serves on the Board of Directors of the Colorado Water Trust, and is a member of Trout Unlimited and the Native Fish Society. He lives in Fort Collins, Colorado.

Introduction

There's a telling interpretative trout display at the Adirondack Wild Center in Tupper Lake, New York. There, biologists have accurately built a trout ecosystem under a closed roof. It's replete with moving water, mimicked natural habitat, macroinvertebrate life on display, and, of course, real-life brook trout native to the region. Amidst all the action there's a brain, well, two brains actually, built life-size from white plastic and jutting out from the side of a blue display aimed at stirring young minds.

Above the larger of the two craniums, it reads: "Angler." Above the tiny one next to it, it reads: "Trout." And the intended irony is glaring.

We humans are able to feel and express emotions. We're able to love. We're able to learn. We're able to operate complex systems and communicate with people across time zones and language barriers. We're able to move freely from Palm Springs summers to Rocky Mountain winters. We have the Internet. We've even explored outer space, for chrissakes. Trout can't do any of that. The display hit like a sucker punch to the gut from a nine-year-old girl.

Next to those two grossly disproportionate brains is another diminutive blue sign with pointed white writing that says, "There are more than 11,000 books for sale telling us how to outsmart trout. See the size of a wild brook trout brain compared to your brain?" It gets worse, "Trout can find their way back to the spot where they hatched without the maps we'd need." More, "They can detect all kinds of things about what they might or might not eat without calling poison control. There is an amazing amount of information in this pea-size brain. Trout can do what they do because they are hardwired to do it."

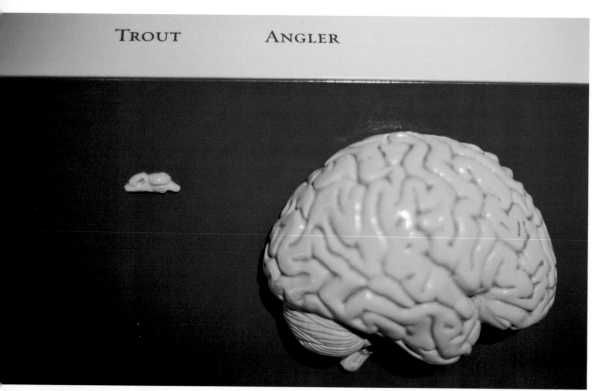

TROUT   ANGLER

Just goes to show, size doesn't always matter. A telling trout vs. human brain comparison from The Wild Center in Upstate New York's Adirondack State Park.

It's a provoking piece of writing, especially considering how smart we *know* we are; and how smart we *actually* are. Before we can even buy books about learning how to catch fish, we must learn how to read them in the first place. Fish on the other hand don't have to read books on how to not get caught by fly fishers, as well as all the predators encountered during a lifetime underwater. They are programmed—from egg to fry to fingerling to juvenile to adult—to be wary. As humans have adapted alongside technology, a lot of day-to-day life has become rather trivial, really—at least from a survival, man vs. savage nature standpoint. Fly fishers catch fish because we derive pleasure from the experience. Fishing is fun, definitely not life and death. And that is where trout have us beat. In general humankind is a fat, lazy, and complacent kind. Computers, remote controls, and way smarter-than-us phones allow us to command a world at our fingertips and on our butts, because it's easier that way. Survival of the fattest, so to speak.

When it comes to fly fishers and all lovers of the great outside in general, however, there is still hope. Despite the lack of hunter-gatherer—"Me must feed Jane!"—urgency to fish, we have grocery stores and delivery to fill those voids; every time a rod is cast and a river perused, we are essentially stepping back into an ancient reality where primal instinct, understanding, and actually being able to think and perform outside a digitized box is vital to success. Nature dictates many of these victories, and on the water it pays to be in unison with what she's saying. In order to source and master this primal language—one

A trout's world is another one altogether—and it's one in constant flux.

pea-brain trout have had dialed since they first set fin on this planet—our story begins underwater.

The underwater cosmos of trout is not a new field of exploration. It is one that has been a highlight of books, hundreds of magazine articles, fish conventions, and confessionals for years: from West Kootenay campfire and last call at Livingston's Murray Bar, to caffeine-driven kitchen conferences at 5:30 a.m. the world over. The quest, the crusade, the investigative days, weeks, and years stolen to decipher quirky trout behavior is the driver behind why we do what we do. And there are occasions where we pick up the scent and follow it through to spectacular results.

With all this help on our side, libraries brimming with on- and in-river anecdotes, blogs, and Google and Wikipedia pages loaded with useful (and sometimes useless) knowledge, there is still no Holy Grail when it comes to sourcing solutions to underwater conundrums. The problem lies in the fact that the trout environment is not a static entity. Instead it is constantly changing, dictated by the current state of environmental upheavals—and this is all taking place faster than it ever has.

Author Malcolm Gladwell coined the phrase "tipping point" in his *New York Times* bestseller, *The Tipping Point: How Little Things Can Make a Big Difference*. A tipping point is basically marked by a buildup of minor changes or incidents that reach a level where they trigger change—either positive or negative. In trout habitat and behavioral terms, tipping points have become increasingly evident—from East Coast to West—in the form of alarming environmental factors. Essentially the underwater trout world, and our interactions with it, has changed so drastically to date that we've been forced to completely rethink our approach to fishing. What trout saw and did, and how they reacted to hatches and shaped feeding behaviors in a free-flowing, pre-dammed Bighorn River, for instance, is not necessarily how they see and act today. The construction of dams and the formation of tailwater fisheries have benefitted trout in many ways. Stabilized flows through four seasons and consistent forage-friendly water temperatures mitigated by bottom flows from lakes and reservoirs have produced remarkable fish factories in their wake. Those fish, however, are not the same fish. Fluctuating water temperature in the spring and fall is a trigger for natural reproduction. Historically browns and rainbows in these systems spawned like clockwork to days on a calendar you could pinpoint year in and year out. Today on many of those same systems, with virtually no rise and fall in seasonal water temperatures, many trout species can be found spawning year-round. What does that mean for you as a fly fisher? You might want to tie on an egg, and leave it on through spring, summer, winter, and fall.

The Elwha River in Washington's Olympic National Park might be the best trout behavioral case study we've seen in contemporary times, demonstrating how human-altered habitats and massive shifts, play out in the fly-fishing field. The Elwha started life as a forested, fern-cloaked Pacific Northwest beauty. But when hydroelectricity generation became a priority it was subsequently plugged for power. Steelhead and runs of massive chinook salmon pushing 100-plus pounds were blocked from their spawning headwaters. Small pockets of resident trout, however, did well sandwiched within their new concrete confines. In 2011, to environmental fanfare, the Glines Canyon and Elwha dams entered into the removal process, the first step to unshackling the river to its free-flowing state. A five-year fishing moratorium has been placed on the Elwha, with the hope that steelhead and various salmon species will return to their natal haunts. How the river might fare between now and then, and how it will be reshaped by the returns of those anadromous runs is a massive question mark currently being studied by area biologists such as NOAA's (National Oceanic and Atmospheric Administration) John McMillan. All we know for certain is that the river will be vastly different, again. The underwater environment will see the flushing of silt—once trapped below the dams—through its long-stagnated gills. Species of macroinvertebrates that had been wiped out with dam construction may or may not return. Resident trout will be forced to compete for spawning space with more robust steelhead and coho salmon. Some of those rainbows and brookies will inevitably perish, while others may thrive with the explosion of incoming nutrients and ramped up forage base from anadromous returns. It's an awesome experiment and, once the dust settles, fly fishers will be forced to adapt—just like the fish.

In addition to dams, rivers continue to be choked by environmental pollutants, aquatic invasive species, unpredictable run-off schedules, massive water withdrawals to feed agricultural interests and cities of thirsty humans, and climate changes that have led to spiked water temperatures and floundering and fluctuating hatch cycles. In some of these systems, trout have been wiped out. In others they have been marginalized to the brink. Yet in many, trout fishing remains good. All of the above scenarios, and how they continue to create seismic shifts in trout life, force fly fishers to rethink their approach. Compounding that, the greater numbers of fly fishers plying increasingly limited resources, while trout are bombarded by new flies and new techniques, ultimately lead to a more educated trout. Remember the pea-brain juxtaposition outlined earlier? Despite our oversize noggins, and often egos, we still clearly have our work cut out for us.

When it comes to solving trout mysteries, there are those who have sunk to great depths to fine-tune their understanding of the underwater world and spread wisdoms to the flock. My enduring bedtime reading pal,

Roderick Haig-Brown, perhaps hit the nail cleanest when he penned these words:

> A fly fisherman's knowledge is compounded of many things. It grows out of imagination, curiosity, bold experiment and intense observation. A fly fisherman must always be picturing to himself what is going on under the water; he must try to understand what his fly means to the fish and so he must choose it or tie it with meaning, he must try to make it move in or on the water with meaning. He must look for new ideas, try them out when they come to him and watch closely to see their effect and find others.

Like Haig-Brown, I have spent a good amount of time obsessing about trout: where they live, what they eat, and how they behave with regard to flies and various presentations—through the simmering days of summer into fall, winter freeze, and spring thaw. They are always close, swimming in the back of the brain as I scramble to lay out *Drake* magazine pages on deadline, or skip out on a Thursday afternoon to shuttle up the Cache la Poudre canyon with equally obsessed fishing friends. You see, in addition to pining for fishing, studying their whereabouts, and obsessing about what flies work and the ones that don't, I fish. I fish a lot. But—disclaimer—I am not a biologist by trade. And I've shaped my writing career around outdoors escapes rooted in conservation, entertainment, and adventure, and less on the science side of the spectrum. This has set up an insatiable quest for information, especially as it pertains to catching more and bigger fish. And my goal with this book is to draw upon top research from all facets of the game and present you, the reader, with a complete and compelling story on underwater trout behavior—from a perspective that takes into account our vast and fast-shifting environments, both above and under the water.

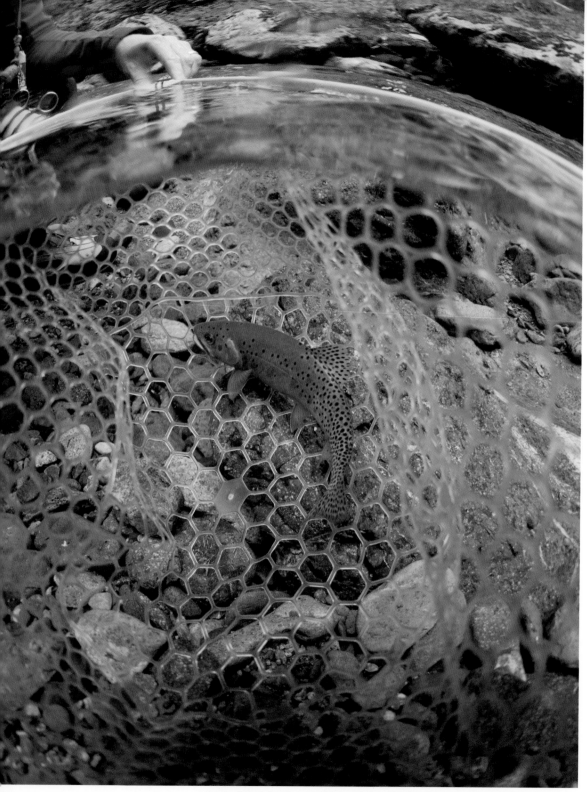

Roderick Haig-Brown wrote that a fly fisher's knowledge grows out of imagination, curiosity, experimentation, and observation. When we apply those thoughts to the underwater world, the hope is to resurface with a new sense of meaning.

As members of the bipedal ranks, we understand fish and the way they function from a human perspective. Our knowledge is based on what's been passed down from friends, family, and mentors; what we've studied in books and magazines; and what we've experienced in our individual river quests. Rarely, however, do we seek to interpret this sport from the point of view of trout. But the old adage "Think like a fish," it turns out, is more than baseless drivel. It's a concept that makes complete sense. For instance, the more you and I can channel our inner fish, understand their instinctual actions as they pertain to seasons in flux, adapt to feeding events, water temperatures, and visual perceptions based on their interpretations—everything from leaders to split-shot to tippet to flies to techniques to wading proximity—the better fishers we become.

The best guides and fishers I know are not necessarily Steve Rajeff distance casters or MIT-trained savants. What they do possess in abundance is fish sense. They know when to find trout (salmon, steelhead, bonefish, tarpon, permit . . .) and where; more importantly, they know what flies to feed them and how. Fish sense often belongs to fly fishers at one with their homewater—that is, those who have accumulated thousands of days rowing rivers in rain, sleet, and snow, all the while producing buckets of fish. Unfortunately (or fortunately, depending on the state of your liver health) we can't all be guides. But we can all take steps to understanding trout in a way that's beneficial to our fly-fishing bottom line. To those who claim they are not in it to catch fish, that's a nice sentiment. But I'm calling bullshit.

. . . .

Playing to trout behavior can be a no-brainer—when the fishing and catching equation clicks seamlessly. But other times it's more complex, our spastic fishing efforts culminating in a dirty shellacking. When it comes down to it, trout do possess pea-size brains, ones that have awesomely kept our melon-shaped craniums captivated and confused since the days of Izaak Walton, when he first visited Charles Cotton's fishing house on the River Dove. But what's been gleaned by researching, writing, and shooting this book, by traveling up and down the great states of Colorado, Wyoming, and Montana, by venturing to the Left Coast, and then to the East, and by fishing and speaking with experts in fish fields ranging from habitat consultants to Washington State steelhead gurus to fisheries biologists to authors, filmmakers, river stewards, aquatic entomologists, and guides—the ones who get it done for clients on 200-plus day seasons— what's been learned and what I aim to present here is the state of human headway in the great catch-up game against trout.

That said, the information contained in this book is aimed to help you catch more trout. But more than catching trout, this book is about understanding trout and why their survival is essential to our fishing. Perhaps, underwater, we can add some insights into man's screwy pursuit to outsmart fish with artificial flies—when we know in our hearts that there's a homerun response contained in the plunk of a wriggling, live worm.

. . . .

A note on photographer Tim Romano:

When I signed on to write a book on the underwater world of trout, I knew that I'd need the help of an expert behind the lens. It's one thing to write and talk about where trout live and feed, but it's a place that's useless without exquisite imagery to take us from mere thought and deliver us to those holds and lairs frequented by fish. Tim Romano is not only an adept fine-arts photographer, but he's also a skilled fly fisher, one who's traveled most of the world in pursuit of perfect shots: those taken from a camera, or those cast to a feeding fish.

Tim and I have fished throughout Colorado and I have written several stories for his *Angling Trade* publication as a contributing editor over the years, but we'd never undergone a project of this magnitude together. Our first meeting upon signing paperwork was in Fort Collins. Tim hauled his boat up from Boulder and the plan was to fish the lower canyon on a raging Poudre River that was cresting at about 3,000 cfs (cubic feet per second). We would float the river then reconvene at a local establishment to discuss business, that is, lining up the best images to coincide with each chapter, which meant planning more fishing trips.

After the first float, with an hour and a half left to get home and meet his wife for dinner, Tim called off our scheduled meeting to rally back to the put-in for one more river lap. Tim got home that night late for dinner, having come close to decapitation when I rowed under a low-lying cable, and with one fish—the only fish landed that day—under his belt. We would have to reschedule beer-in-hand book meetings for another time. But right then and there I knew Tim was the man for the job.

Geoff Mueller
Fort Collins, Colorado

1 Born to Swim

Life moves pretty fast. If you don't stop and look around once in a while, you could miss it.

—Ferris Bueller,
Ferris Bueller's Day Off

Since they first laid fin on this continent, trout were born to swim. According to Robert J. Behnke's book, *Trout and Salmon of North America*, the first "perhaps" progenitor of salmon and trout was *Eosalmo*, which swam the arteries of the Pacific Northwest 50 million years ago.

Other salmonids came to the Rocky Mountain region and joined the mix about 30 million years ago. Fifteen million years later, Pleistocene glaciers retreated, leaving cold mountain streams and alpine lakes. About a million years ago, ancestors of all contemporary cutthroat populated the Columbia and Snake rivers and their tributaries. And approximately 10,000 years ago, they breached the basins of the Platte, Arkansas, and Rio Grande, marking the rise of contemporary cutthroat trout. Today, various trout species—both native and nonnative—extend a wide underwater shadow, inhabiting coldwater haunts from the headwaters of Bristol Bay, east to Europe and Asia, and south through the wind-torn Tierra del Fuego region.

All these trout share in common an uncanny ability to swim and survive, despite a growing list of habitat shifts and ecological adversities. What makes a trout a trout is a complex equation of many variables that have been fine-tuned through evolution. Moreover, trout have adapted and adopted specific traits that have optimized their ability to thrive in cold, freshwater environs—the pristine lakes, rivers, and streams they call home.

Freshwater salmonids, including species such as rainbow, brown, brook, lake, cutthroat, and bull trout, all share similar defining characteristics. A trout's streamlined, torpedo-shaped body, its distinct colorations, fin placement, and signaling lateral lines all serve nuanced purposes that go above and beyond the general esthetics and beauty that continue to bewitch fly fishers. Trout are born with gills in which to breathe. Gill filaments are covered by a thin membrane, which absorbs oxygen from the water and releases carbon dioxide back into it. Gill arches consist of rakers, which strain food such as zooplankton and other microscopic particles from the water. Inside the outer facade, a trout's engine is driven by many of the same organs found in vertebrates. But according to Behnke, there are significant anatomical anomalies stemming from life underwater, as opposed to life above it. Trout have hearts to pump blood, kidneys and livers to process waste, a stomach and intestine for digestion purposes, and testes and ovaries for reproduction. A trout's air bladder, unique to fishes, extends the entire length of its body cavity, and filled with gas it provides buoyancy and stability in the water. It's also sensitive to changing environmental factors such as barometric pressure, which can throw a wrench in feeding routines.

Encompassing the outer fuselage, fins—many of them—characterize trout, including dorsal, adipose, caudal (or tail), anal, pelvic, and pectoral fins. These appendages in combination with compact muscles that extend the entire length of a trout's body, drive both speed and stability underwater. The top speed of a rainbow trout is approximately 20 mph, for instance. And wild trout are faster than their inferior, hatchery-incubated brethren. A trout's streamlined build also gives it the ability to take flight, to pluck a mayfly from the air or spit a foul-tasting

A trout's façade is characterized by fins—many of them. Fins in combination with compact muscles provide the thrust to outmaneuver both predator and prey.

hook. When it comes back to gravity, trout use pelvic and pectoral fins to return to right-side up and regain footing in the river.

While fins and muscle give trout flight and thrust, from a purely fish-catching perspective, understanding how sensory organs work in relation to trout behavior is paramount. Sensory organs are essential to trout navigation. And more than moving from point A to point B, they provide a map for living. Fish do not breathe through their nostrils (or nares); they have gills for that. Instead, trout take in water over nasal sacs, which allow them to "smell" their way through migratory systems, while also aiding in reproduction and feeding. Using smell as a cue,

Behnke tells us that some chemical compounds elicit a greater response than others. And although the effect of unkempt wading boots has yet to be fully analyzed, it's safe to say that a whiff of "human" is not high on a trout's list of favorite smells.

Since most of us aren't "chumming" for takes—or clinching on scented baits when our fishing partners aren't looking—a trout's senses of hearing and sight take the main stage in our catching pursuits. Fish don't have external ears, but they are listening. In fact, sound travels much faster underwater than it does through the air, about five times quicker and, as explored in later chapters, it plays a role in how close we can get to fish without spooking them . . . sometimes. In addition to a sense of hearing, all trout have a highly receptive lateral line system, which allows them to feel—everything from movement and sound to pressure changes and the chemical composition of their underwater environment. Lateral lines amplify a trout's ability to hear and see: for instance, when visibility is poor due to turbid water or in the crashing currents of a fast-flowing riffle. Lateral lines also contribute to a trout's overall wariness, wherever it resides in the water.

A trout's sense of sight is another tool of deft, specialized engineering. We know that trout see color and can discern the shape and size of our best fly imitations. But more than that, Behnke writes, "Trout and salmon have very accurate vision over a rather wide range and even possess the ability to focus on objects that are very close, while clearly seeing distant objects at the same time." A trout's eye is designed to detect motion and focus and it plays an essential role in its feeding, and our fishing. Trout also have both binocular and monocular vision. The former allows them to see in front of them, while the latter gives them a side-view mirror glimpse to what's beside and behind. Trout not only see what's underwater, but eye placement high on the head gives

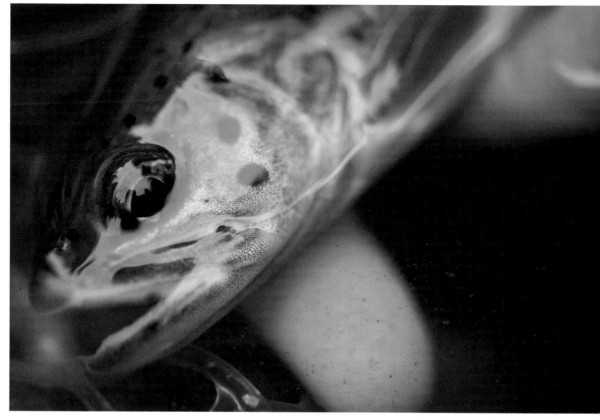

The trout's eye is a remarkable, specialized sensory tool—giving cutthroat trout (above) the ability to detect motion as well as home in and identify both what's in and above the water.

them a dome-like view of what's above. This allows trout to home in on emerging mayflies or dropping spinners, while simultaneously spying and avoiding telltale predatory signs, such as Simms logos and red trucker hats. A trout's central nervous system, including its brain and spinal cord, is the computer behind the chaos— providing the means to process and react instinctually to the reams of sensory beta processed on a dusk-thru-dawn basis.

Taking into account the above variables, there is no denying that trout possess an exceptional design, and it's this simple, elegant engineering that makes them built to swim better than most. Clunky humans, on the other hand—confined to breaststrokes, back crawls, Pabsts, and blow-up inner tubes—comparatively suck at this. [Michael Phelps, Kevin Costner (in *Waterworld*), and the Swampthing not included, but as an overall populous, fish we are not.] If trout can reach speeds upwards of 20 mph, the fastest all-star swimmers on team human, such as Phelps, might push 6 mph, max. So it's a good thing catching trout is not a matter of speed. The fact that it's a matter of cunning bodes better, considering our bigger brains. But subtracting human ego and stubbornness, and adding a trout's instinctual wit and wariness, the man vs. fish fracas sort of evens out. Some days we win; some we lose.

. . . .

The question then becomes: How can we succeed more and fail less? Researching this book and taking fly fishing to the trout cosmos with snorkel and mask has made for some eye-opening revelations in this department. And Utah's Green River, below Flaming Gorge Dam, is as good a place as any to start—a fishery where seeing the overall picture comes into focus much easier than others.

The Green is an apropos name for the sinuous tailwater that has existed below Flaming Gorge Dam since dam construction was completed in the 1960s. The river, once brown with seasonal spats of run-off and loaded with sediment, is now for the most part cool, clear, electric green, and brimming with bugs and trout through four seasons. Based on those criteria, Tim Romano and I chose the Green to commence our underwater R&D in the spring of 2012. We rallied a crew together, and for about a week leading up to our eventual dunking, anxiously watched a dismal forecast showing a Pacific Northwest front pushing south and set to saddle our fishing days. Unfortunately, the onset of spring on the Green does not present optimal swimming conditions. When we booked, it was a balmy 70°F in Fort Collins. I arrived in Dutch John in shorts and flip-flops, and left in layers of fleece, long underwear, and mittens. Water temperatures were a consistent 39 degrees, and although the sun was shining at 10 a.m. on day one, the sky would eventually curdle and turn black—pegging us with hail, thunder, rain, and 60-mph winds.

Despite the jacked weather, we were stoked to acquaint ourselves with the Green's big browns and rainbows from underwater. That included spending ample time with the fish that have spurred and shunned so many of our presentations, as well as ones that have, on occasion, rewarded those efforts. Fish can be discerning one minute and the next, totally reckless. By diving in we were searching for a better handle on why. More specifically,

The author suiting up for a swim during an early, early spring mission on Utah's Green River below Flaming Gorge Dam. The water clarity on this renowned tailwater is about as good as it gets. You see the fish and, without a doubt, they see you, too.

we wanted to find out what triggers or deters trout from eating. What are their tolerance levels to human presence? Which flies work, and when? How much leader, tippet, and split-shot is too much? What characteristics make up the best lies from below, and what does that water look like from above? Does swimming with fish give us a better understanding, a trout's-eye view so to speak, into this whole business of fly fishing? And, moreover, in a dam-everything era, what do humans look like to trout? Have trout lost their fear instinct, becoming lazier, and less sharp? Here they are; and there we were. It was time to suit up and find out.

The A section of the Green, from put-in to Little Hole, runs 7 miles and holds upwards of 20,000 fish per river mile. In addition to a ton of fish, its runs are more penetrable to the human eye than almost any other powerhouse tailwater in the Lower 48, which is great for underwater work. Observing trout from a drift boat or standing from any rock along the foot of Red Canyon, the Green's flows are highly revealing. At the same time it can be a tough SOB when what you see doesn't click with your fishing game plan. According to Steve Schmidt of Western Rivers Flyfisher in Salt Lake City, "The Green is truly one of the best dry-fly fisheries in this country; excellent aquatic hatches, and an abundance of diverse terrestrials create very consistent dry-fly fishing throughout much of the season." It owes this to its cool, consistent water flows and an abundance of bug life that runs the gamut from annelids, cicadas, beetles, and hoppers all the way down to micromayflies and the midges that keep trout on top during "balmy" February and March afternoons. These characteristics also make the Green an ideal place to dunk your head underwater in order to gain some needed fly-fishing perspective.

Eddying out below a run in the A section, our entourage consisted of three drift boats and a raft holding a cast of fiends and friends, including veteran Green guru Schmidt.

Dog's best friend releases girl's favorite fish. Kat Yarbrough and Mikey the dog tangle with a hefty Green River rainbow in the name of critical fly-fishing research.

We packed lunches, dry suits, masks, snorkels, and elbow and kneepads for Tim, underwater camera housings, fins, and a couple of flasks of whiskey to keep warm when we popped up for air. Although it was early season by northern Rockies' standards, winter midges had been cohabitating the river alongside the season's first large Baetis hatches. The days leading up to and during the trip were marked by midges on the water early, Baetis spicing the soup bowl during an 11 a.m. to about 2 p.m. window, and consistent streamer fishing with black, tan, or olive bugs. Accordingly, fish were on the feed. They hammered foam-back RS2s through the morning hours and switched tastes to #18 Baetis nymphs, Soft-Hackles, and drys as the hatch progressed then slowed in late afternoon.

We set up professional test caster, Kat Yarbrough, at the head of a shallow run that dropped into a deep trough and cliff-lined back eddy along the downstream bank. With no rise activity, the rig included a black yarn indicator, two No. 4 split-shots, and a three-foot leader tapering to 5X fluoro tippets. Our trout instigators included two flies: a #18 Jujubaetis and a #22 RS2. Fly choice was easy. The goal was to cover both midge and mayfly hatches, which were prolific and the only game on the water. In the name of results, Kat cast into the verde and began hooking a mix of browns and 'bows in the 14- to 16-inch range on the midge, while two much larger swimming dorks lurked below, shooting photos, and taking notes on the play-by-play.

With morning midges above and below the surface, Kat's midge out-produced its Baetis counterpart by about 5 to 1. Eliminating the Baetis and fishing two midge patterns further increased catch rates. Although Baetis nymphs were evident on the river bottom, midges were the breakfast preference, which was not surprising considering their overall abundance at this time in the river (more on energy expenditure and its relation to caloric return, later). Consistently, when Baetis came to life around noon, tables turned, midges became yesterday's meatloaf, and the larger (#18) mayfly eatery ramped up through the hatch cycle.

From underwater looking up, the strike indicator was evident, although ginked black yarn rode high and produced less splash or wake than Thingamabobbers and other hard-foam indicators. With the sun rising over the canyon wall, light penetration through the water was brilliant. What looked like contrasting shades of buttery yellows to rich greens, browns, blacks, and tans from above showed up much flatter and filtered through the mask underwater. Trout can see color well, but they see it differently than humans—including UV and infrared light, which we can't see at all. With our heads buried inside the moving river, color was relatively static across the board, and instead of the variety we saw from above, shadows and contrasting light conditions were more evident than actual greens, yellows, and blacks below. Dark greens and blacks above indicated moss covered rock and deep recesses underwater. Light, glowing greens above produced scoured rocks in fast-water seams and riffles. And light yellows above showed sand-bottom depressions, perfect habitat for ascending midges and midging browns and rainbows. In addition to structure and bottom contours, leaders, tippets, split-shots and anything attached to fly line and fly fisher were also apparent to us and are undoubtedly seen by trout, too. Despite the Green's noted clarity through the surface,

Trout are generally not spooked by this view— instead they acclimate quickly to the presence of finned foreigners. They are, however, smarter than you might think when it comes to interpreting the merit of a #22 midge that misses the mark.

from underwater we were amazed at how laden it was with particulate matter. In bright conditions, anything natural or unnatural was illuminated—from the smallest mayfly and midge imitations to the natural drift minutiae coursing within the river's pulse.

This section of the Green, as stated, is also stacked with trout, making them relatively easy to spot. But what was more impressive than sheer numbers, perhaps, was their tolerance for two doofs flopping around in dry suits. Swimming with trout, it turns out, is actually a lot easier than fishing for them. As long as they weren't brushed with our plastic fins and protruding body parts, we weren't perceived as much of a threat. Probably because in this pathetic state of immobility, we weren't. Less tolerant trout, the ones that didn't appreciate the intrusion of buggy eyes and mouth spouts, still eventually acclimated to our presence.

At a pushy 3,000 cfs, plenty of fish were observed. And although they were eating, most were glued to the bottom, stationary and inactive other than the opening and closing of gums as water filtered through gills and food channeled into stomachs. Because of the river's low temps, fish hooked by Kat scored low in the piss-and-vinegar department and high in lethargic response. They came fast to shore for handshakes and skilled portraiture before being released back into the drink. Trout metabolism essentially hibernates in the winter in the name of storing food energy during drawn out, nonfeeding conditions. These fish were on the rebound, with ramped up hatches about to enter the mix. As the water temperatures continue to climb through spring and early summer, so would their strength, body mass, and activity levels.

. . . .

One of the more impressive notables contained within the whole underwater experience is witnessing the dynamics that make a trout a trout. Engaging fish on an even playing field, without a rod and as just another swimming being, is telling. Trout hold effortlessly in currents that we would work hard to stay stationary in for more than thirty seconds in a bulky dry suit. Trout, obviously, are able to breathe underwater, where we require a snorkel and steady stream of oxygen to stay conscious. Trout are keenly aware of their surroundings through lateral lines and air bladders, and by way of honed senses such as hearing, smell, and sight. I, on the other hand, looking up from a 20-inch brown stuck to the bottom of the river, nearly ran headfirst into a rock wall. Trout are cold-blooded and DNA-programmed to change their metabolic function and adapt behaviors appropriately in

A trout's ability to swim is a gift that's suited it well for eons. And while we humans are comparatively awkward at these underwater endeavors, swimming with trout provides eye-opening perspective to those who strive to think like fish.

Tools for Taking the Plunge

Swimming with trout is a much easier proposition than actually catching trout, so long as you come prepared.

Dry Suits. Dry suits are not a necessity for underwater business. But they are a luxury, especially when water temperatures plummet below 60°F. With neck, wrist, and ankle gaskets, you will stay dry and, depending on how well you layer, warm. The main difference between dry suits and wet suits is spelled out in the name. Dry suits block water from entering. This generally allows for better insulation, making them more suitable for use in cold water. Lastly, dry suits are expensive. If you want to save money—and avoid the onset of hypothermia—wait till summer and go commando.

Hoods and Gloves. Trout are cold-blooded and do much better in cold-water temperatures than humans. Neoprene hoods and gloves help trap heat against your head and hands during extended sessions. The thicker the neoprene, 5 mm vs. 3 mm, for instance, the longer you will endure underwater when it's cold. Go lighter for warmer water snorkeling.

Masks and Snorkels. A well-fitting mask is essential to seeing trout underwater. Not only does it protect your eyes, but it also opens them to your new surroundings. When shopping for a mask, hold it up to your face and breathe in through your nose. The mask should form a stay-put seal, without painful pressure points on the bridge of your nose, forehead, or sides of the face. Snorkels: If you're running the river without an oxygen tank, a snorkel will at least keep you in the game longer, lurking underwater.

Weight Belts. Weight belts can be rented from most dive shops. If your goal is to get deep, added weight is essential. Dry suits trap air and keep you buoyant. Weight belts combat this effect.

Cameras and Underwater Housings. Most cameras we know don't like water. For shooting this book Tim Romano used a Nikon D700 and a variety of lenses, including a 16 mm f2.8, 20 mm f2.8, 20-35 mm f2.8, and a 50 mm f1.4. His Ikelite housing is waterproof to 200 feet and consists of a modular port system with an 8-inch acrylic dome. Tim recommends always tethering your housing to your body via a quick-release cord. If you drop it, it's going to sink fast. Never place your housing in the direct sun if possible; this contributes to massive amounts of camera-wrecking condensation when you dunk your housing in cold water. Be cognizant of grit and dirt on your port dome and any part of your housing. This can scratch the plastic, making shooting difficult. Re-lube and check O-rings for nicks or cuts prior to every dive.

Places to Find Trout/Avoid Disturbing Fishers. Not all water types are equal when it comes to swimming with trout—especially if your hope is to see them. Trout require cool, clear, oxygenated water to survive, and varied habitat is essential to that equation. Thus, when you're looking for trout underwater, look for habitat that is conducive to holding trout but is also large enough to hold a couple of lunker humans, without scattering every fish in the run or pool. For shooting and observing fish, target large, deep, slow-moving pools—or stillwaters. Fast, oxygenated water makes seeing fish more difficult. On the other hand, you will often get closer to the fish in these scenarios because the water carries more noise, making sneaking up from above or below easier. Time of year is another key consideration for swimming with trout. Pre-run-off can be cold, but it presents good water clarity, while run-off and even post-run-off can turn the picture ultrafuzzy with turbidity. Tailwaters help eliminate this problem, offering more consistent flows. And some are better than others, as are some freestones. Many of the best tailwaters we fish are not necessarily clear. The North Platte system in Wyoming, for instance. And many of the better swimming freestones we know are so spectacularly crystalline you can see clear through the deepest runs on the blackest days. With that in mind, it's essential to know your rivers, talk to locals who have fished them recently, and keep close tabs on weather and water conditions. Lastly, many of our favorite rivers are filled with fly fishers, especially during prime hatch events. If you plan on swimming with trout, choose times and river sections that allow you to get away from the crowds. No one wants you swimming through a pod of rising rainbows when they've driven several hours to catch a fish. Respect the resource, as well as your fellow fishers.

cool water temps. After an hour or so in the same water, I quickly lost sense of all senses, including any feeling in my hands, feet, and face.

The trout's ability to swim effortlessly is a strength. For humans it's not even close. As a kid I got by with a mean doggy paddle, and never scored higher than a maroon badge at the local rec center. This didn't really matter because I preferred sitting in the hot tub, which was a much more enjoyable way to work up a sweat. I also liked to ski, and to this day swimming up to my eyeballs in powder beats the shrinkage effect of plunging heels-over-head into a river frozen in winter's icy grip. Trout were born to swim. Humans were born to live on land. But, yes, many of us were also born to fish. And

Photographer Tim Romano equipped for battle with sub-50 degree water temps in early spring on a large Western tailwater. Note: Dry suits, multiple layers, masks, and neoprene hoods and gloves all keep blood flowing to the brain . . . so long as your neck gasket isn't riding too tight.

although we can't swim like trout, by swimming with trout we heighten our understanding of their habits and habitat—ultimately making us better fishers. Knowing where fish hunker during frosty river temps on a tailwater in springtime flows is the kind of knowledge that drives results. And knowing when to feed trout Baetis over midges by merely looking at a watch doesn't hurt either. Over the course of four seasons on the river during various feeding events that mark the year, bringing the underwater world to the surface changes the way we fish—for the better.

2 Trout Intel

Designing the Fly Fisher's Fish

Everyone is a genius. But if you judge a fish on its ability to climb a tree, it will live its whole life believing that it is stupid.

—Albert Einstein

The road is a single-lane switchback that cuts through a large-scale industrial copper and molybdenum mine in south central British Columbia. The yellow gates are freshly painted and hold heavy-duty locks. The keys fit. But we—a couple of fly fishers towing a 16-foot jon boat—don't. We drag the rig to the water's edge and launch in a pea-green soup of algae in bloom and the sun-bleached shucks of already hatched bugs. If someone were to say they regularly hauled double-digit rainbows from this manmade hole in the ground, I'd be skeptical. But if that someone were British Columbia biologist and guide Brian Chan, I'd be in the truck helping open and close those cumbersome yellow gates at 6 a.m. on a Sunday morning.

"Geoff," Brian had told me prior to flying west for a week of fishing in British Columbia's Kamloops region, "I've got some water I want you to see." Brian and I had fished a handful of lakes throughout the Okanagan on similar occasions. But I'd been familiar with at least most of the stillwaters we'd hit. If I hadn't, they were easy enough to scour online or on a map. This destination was different. "It's the Ministry's test lake," Brian said, "and it's loaded with massive Blackwater strain rainbows."

For gawking purposes my curiosities had been piqued with a handful of graphic Frankentrout pictures. But more than the visual stimuli, I was intrigued by what I might ultimately learn casting #14 chironomids into the heart of the province's freshwater fisheries petri dish. Catching trout is more often than not an exercise for experience, adventure, and euphoria delivered by a heavy dose of nature on your 9-to-5 brain. But fishing—and fisheries management—is also about science, especially when it comes to testing behavioral hypothesis on trout in their underwater environs. Fishing "Test Lake" was more than a chance at big fish. It meant immersion

British Columbia still-water expert Brian Chan peruses the chironomid box in preparation for the first light bite on Roche Lake.

Photo by Geoff Mueller

in a grand experiment that British Columbia's fisheries departments have been studying, documenting, tallying results, and implementing management strategies for best-catch scenarios since the late 1940s.

In the early 1950s, the province birthed its provincial Fish and Wildlife Commission, tasking biologists to expand its recreational fish management reach through enhanced stocking efforts. The province's first stocks came from wild rainbow populations in the Paul, Shuswap, and Pennask Lakes. The latter, located between the central interior hubs of Kamloops and Kelowna, formed the backbone of this fish propagation program. Pennask Lake has never been stocked, but its transplanted brood have fertilized far and wide across a province housing more than 360,000 square miles of lake-potholed land, with more than 20,000 lakes all told. British Columbia's contemporary stocking program includes 825 lakes, which hold approximately 7.5 million trout.

Pennask rainbows stem from the redband species (*Oncorhynchus mykiss gairdneri*) native to the Columbia River Basin. These ancestral redbands likely entered Pennask during glaciation meanderings that marked the Ice Age period, part of an evolutionary sequence in North America that stems back more than 50 million years. To put this epic journey in perspective, fly fishers—of the *Homo sapiens*-brand—have existed for a few hundred years. Trout-like fishes of the family Salmonidae, however, have inhabited the freshwater swirls of Earth since tyrannosaurus rex. As for understanding trout's place in this world in human terms, it's been a long game of catch-up. Robert J. Behnke, one of the world's preeminent trout taxonomists, writes in his book, *Trout and Salmon of North America,* "To comprehend the evolutionary history of trout and salmon, one must take a perspective completely removed from ordinary human experience. One must think not only in millions of years, but in tens and even hundreds of millions of years."

Photo by Geoff Mueller

Pennask rainbows are native to the Columbia River Basin. Today they can be found throughout the productive Kamloops area stillwater circuit.

Those are a lot of zeros to fathom. What we do know about Pennask trout—as well as its close Blackwater River relatives—is that these fish are prone to eat, much like fat kids waddling into cafeteria lines on Pizza Friday. They aggressively eat other forage fish and insects. They bulk up fast on protein. And they are prone to take flies, making them a perfect cultured fish, which is the reason they have become integral components of BC's provincial stocking program.

What makes the ultimate trout from a fisheries perspective? According to Chan, it's the fish—a catchable one—that can survive and thrive best in its allotted space. "What really sets BC apart as far as lake fishing are its monoculture lakes—lakes with no competing species that just hold rainbow trout," Chan explains. "Usually the insect base and other aquatic life is very prolific, so we like to select strains of fish that are insectivores, like Pennask."

For the purpose of this discussion, it's important to note that not all lakes—or rivers—are equal. When monocultures become muddied, and where a diverse mix of competing species exists, piscivorous trout that eat and take advantage of all available food sources are the preferred quarry. At Stump Lake, located just outside Kamloops, for instance, back-to-back low water years caused deathly spikes in pH and alkalinity in the early 2000s. Stump also has a high population of prickly sculpins, fish

In spring and extending through the summer season, rivers aren't the only entities affected by healthy snowpack. Many Western stillwaters are dependent on spring run-off to revitalize the water table—regulating pH and alkalinity levels.

its resident rainbows ignore. The ideal fish for this distinct environment? Lahontan cutthroat. At least that's what local fisheries professionals are banking on. Lahontans are piscivorous by nature. They also thrive in water with elevated pH levels, or lakes that get too salty for some species of trout to properly osmoregulate. When osmoregulation shuts down, trout suffer an ionic unbalance in their bloodstream, which leads to mortality. This is a common occurrence in Western stillwaters during extended seasons of drought. Healthy winter snowpack levels followed by a wet spring help recharge the water table, reducing both pH and alkalinity to trout-friendly levels. Osmoregulation is ramped up. Trout thrive.

When it comes to catching these fish, whether it's a pH-tolerant Lahontan, an insect-prone Pennask, a whirling disease-resistant Hofer-cross, or a piscivorous Blackwater rainbow, trout are only as smart as the inherited traits they possess on a species-specific level. Understanding these traits helps make you a savvier fisher, but unfortunately it doesn't make trout any dumber.

A commonly held definition of intelligence is the ability to reason, solve problems, think abstractly, comprehend complex ideas, learn quickly, and learn from experience. Humans (most) have got this. Dolphins? Pretty close. Trout?

In Euan Macphail's *Brain and Intelligence in Vertebrates*, the author contrasts dolphin intelligence with big-brain elephants in a race for non-human cranial supremacy. Flipper, it turns out, is the PhD candidate of the Underwater University. Dolphins understand advanced concepts such as numerical continuity and are great mimickers and trick learners. Although we won't see trout performing double gainers at Sea World anytime soon, they too can be understood—or better misunderstood—in terms of Macphail's research when he states: "The true extent of [a species'] intelligence is really unknown to humans in the sense that we, ourselves, have evolved over time to maintain sustenance on the land whereas they have evolved to live in the water."

Trout, like dolphins and other finned species, have evolved to live in water, which makes the dry land-based fly fisher's task that much more difficult. We theorize in our cars on the way to work. Trout, on the other hand, work to stay alive in a different world of rock nooks and river hydraulics. We sip whiskey and tie flies on tying vises in our living rooms and dens. The result looks trouty enough to us, but what it looks like to an actual trout is more complex. When it comes to trout smarts, Chan says, "All we can say by doing creel surveys is that some trout are extremely aggressive feeders. You can translate that into willingness to bite. For instance in test fisheries where we differentiate Pennask fish with fin clips, we often see that Blackwaters make up the majority of the catch." This is because they've maintained their aggressive feeding behavior, which stems from a highly competitive environment. "Those traits get passed on to their progeny—that's why we call them 'gullible.'"

What can we deduce from this? It's evident that certain strains of trout are more gullible (or catchable) than others, based on genetics and immediate environmental factors such as competition and forage base. But trout, like Flipper, haven't survived this long on earth because they are stupid. In general, trout behavior is reactionary and survival based. They either see a fly and eat; or they don't. They see tippet spray and line slap from an errant cast and a looming unnatural shadow and bolt; or they gorge happily for hours . . . undisturbed. There is not a ton of Freudian theory involved in this equation. And, moreover, as fishers our goal is to produce a reaction that leads to a positive outcome, whereby the fish acts accordingly and the puzzle is one step closer to solved.

Back at Test Lake laboratories, where despite a couple of jumped fish our supposedly "gullible" Blackwaters are mostly bruising our egos, Chan tells me that close

Not-so-gullible cutthroat. This Rocky Mountain National Park mainstay is reputed to crush terrestrials and come quick to hand. This little guy bucked the trend, preferring to sip microscopic pseudos during an early-summer hatch.

examination of angler traffic around the Kamloops area has helped biologists better understand the cause-and-effect relationship between fish and fishers. On Kamloops's Roche Lake, for instance, which sees enough aluminum boats launched into its depths each trout season to qualify for smelting status, fly fishers make up the brunt of fishing pressure. And trout acclimate quickly to the bobber brigade's wiggling-carrot approach of chironomids and midge patterns under Day-Glo strike-indicators. Here with an imprecise hatch match, Chan says, you won't catch many fish. But if you turned the clock back twenty-five years on Roche, "and had the same fishing conditions with heavy hatches, you could have gotten away with fishing a black and silver chirono-mid and caught tons of fish. . . all day."

We, unfortunately, live in busier fishing times. And trout are smarter, or at least evolution has prepro-grammed them to react more frugally in situations that involve the sharp prick of honed hooks. Biologists are certain that the combination of seeing hundreds of pat-terns, and having been routinely caught and released, provokes a learned response in trout. In other words, they have been reprogrammed to avoid certain food items that aren't quite natural. Hammered fish are more prone to these "gun-shy" qualities. But there's more to the intelligence debate. On Test Lake, which remains largely unpressured thanks to those shiny locked yellow gates, Chan and I finally land a couple. We stomach pump two fish, produce flies that closely resemble the regurgitated midges, yet still failed miserably. A week after returning home, Chan writes me with this explanation: "Found out why the fishing was slow, the mine pumped 18 inches of water into it earlier in the week. That mixed the lake and definitely put the fish off the bite in large part and also increased the algal bloom. Friends fished it on the Friday and they got skunked!!"

It's always a reassuring ego stroke to know you're not the only ones not catching. More than that, however, fish-ing is a constant quest for answers. And those answers often come well after we exit the water.

Mini-marbles with one telling trait—eyes. Hatchery bound rainbow
trout eggs already in the process of developing their sense of sight,
which they'll use to home in on the daily pellet hatch before moving
into Colorado's free-flowing Poudre River.

3 Trout: A Lifetime in an Evolving River Environment

Case Study: Colorado's Cache la Poudre River

A fly fisherman must always be picturing to himself what is going on under the water; he must try to understand what his fly means to the fish and so he must choose it or tie it with meaning. He must look for new ideas, try them out when they come to him and watch closely to see their effect and find others.

—Roderick Haig-Brown, *A River Never Sleeps*

The human embryo, even at six week's gestation, looks amazingly *human*-like—albeit a really small one contained within a large, gooey bubble. Its distinct head encompasses a developing brain, towering over a diminutive body that would cradle neatly in the palm of your hand.

The trout version, in comparison, is pretty simplistic. In fact what's going on inside the ovum doesn't resemble anything much like a trout at all. Roll around a brown trout or rainbow egg, prod it with your fingers, and inspect it closely. There is no visible tail, no fins, gill plates, mandibles, or shimmering scales contained within. But these bright, misshapen marbles are punctuated by something telling: large, piercing black eyes, especially as they get closer to hatching. This telltale marker will become essential when it comes to the next twelve months in the river. Trout need to see food, in order to eat food, in order to survive. Simple. The eyes say it all.

Before trout eggs can sprout beady black eyes, and everything else that goes into becoming viable river prodigies, we must take into account the natural reproduction phenomenon known as the spawn. Rainbow, brown, cutthroat, and brook trout spawn in main river channels, headwaters, tributaries, and inlet or outlets of lakes. In the spring and early summer, rainbows concentrate spawning activities in gravel-bottomed tailouts.

As seasons in northern latitudes transcend from summer to fall and early winter, it's the browns turn to get busy. And on northern Colorado's Cache la Poudre River—a Front Range rivulet that rushes eastward out of the Rocky Mountains through Roosevelt National Forest and emerges in the foothills near the city of Fort Collins—the brown spawn is really the only show in town. Like many rivers throughout the state, many of the Poudre's natal rainbow trout were wiped out by whirling disease in the early '90s. Whirling disease was introduced to the US in Pennsylvania in 1956. It was brought to Colorado when the state traded its rainbows for German browns—of Deutschland proper—to stock in its lakes and rivers. That fish swap would be a disastrous one on several levels. What the pesky Europeans failed to mention—or what the US fish hatchery proponents failed to do their due diligence on—came delivered in the form of a fish epidemic, one carried by sexy German imports in the form of whirling disease spores. Once in the river, these spores were subsequently transferred from stocked waterways as aquatic hitchhikers, latching onto waterfowl, as well as water fouling anglers on boots, waders, and other gear items. Infected trout in the Poudre developed debilitating deformities of the skull and spinal column. Most of the young, wild rainbow trout died shortly after infection. Colorado Division of Wildlife (CDOW) researchers eventually determined that rainbow trout, brook trout, and all of Colorado's native subspecies of cutthroat trout were highly susceptible to whirling disease when exposed as juveniles. But efforts to stymie it came too late.

As far as the Poudre is concerned, what was once a 60:40 rainbow to brown trout split has been turned on its head with the addition of whirling disease to the system. Today, even with a heavy stocking of crossbred, disease-resistant trout by the Colorado Division of Wildlife, biologists have mostly struck out in their efforts to re-establish the naturally reproducing rainbows of yesteryear. The German-engineered browns, however, are still clocking on the miles, in healthy numbers.

In the fall of 2011, I dropped in at one of the Cache la Poudre River's city limits stretches for an inside glimpse at post-whirling disease trout dynamics within the system

A melee of rainbow juveniles destined for the Cache la Poudre River system. Colorado Division of Wildlife biologists are currently working to re-establish naturally reproducing stocks that were wiped out by the whirling disease epidemic of the 1990s.

and, in particular, to study the complex relationships between introduced rainbows and naturally reproducing browns. On a brisk November morning at Lee Martinez Park, CDOW biologist Kurt Davies and his team—as well as this fishing journalist—substituted rods for electrically charged river prods in order to load a few buckets full of trout.

Common sense tells you to keep your fingers out of electrical sockets and away from downed wires. It might also sway you from situations that involve standing in a river while injecting it with a heavy dose of live current. But when it comes to electro-fishing, common sense is nonsense, so long as you adhere to a strict policy of not falling in. With rubber gloves and shaky knees I listened intently to the brief safety spiel then huddled with my posse of seasoned vets on the bank to discuss the play. Davies proceeded to bark orders and we filed into formation in the knee-deep water—as I played clean-up with a yellow-handled net a safe distance downstream of the action. When the whistle blew, our line advanced on a tailout stretch and began the upstream march through an array of fishy looking bends, runs, pockets, and riffle habitats, anywhere we might sack a waylaid trout. As we worked upriver, the temporarily shocked browns and 'bows turned belly-up, and we scooped them with nets and dropped them into watery bins so they could be measured, counted, and returned to the river later that afternoon.

At day's end, our electrofishing score showed healthy numbers of small—less than 16-inch—browns and rainbows. The split between the two species closely resembled the river in its pre-whirling disease form—a return to the days of old on paper, but a highly stocker-subsidized incarnation. The rainbows, for instance—whirling disease-resistant strains of Harrison and Colorado River crossed with German Hofers—were all of the pen-bred variety: incubated and raised at CDOW's Fort Collins-area

Photo by Geoff Mueller

Although rainbow reproduction in Colorado's Poudre River is next to nil, wild brown trout continue to thrive as evidenced by autumn redds such as this one.

hatcheries. But the browns we shocked, more than 500 in this short stretch of water, were of the river-bred variety, an impressive and growing self-sustaining population.

Midway through our first sweep, in the dregs of a large tailout, we carefully navigated around two large redds, gleaming depressions in the cobblestone near where we shocked two of the larger hen browns of the day—both in the 15-inch range. These adult browns began their life in a similar redd environment, as tiny rolling ova, with those piercing black eyes open to fresh discovery.

Every fall on the Poudre, as well as in healthy wild-trout fisheries throughout the West, female browns bend their fiery bright bodies and wave undulating tails to excavate depressions in the gravel called redds. (Brown and brook trout are generally fall and early winter spawners, while rainbow, cutthroat, golden, and Apache trout generally spawn during late winter to spring. Again, water temperature is key to this timing and on tailwater rivers such as Montana's Missouri and Bighorn, where temperature fluctuation is minimal due to mitigation by bottom-release dams, spawn time—for a mix of species—can mean any time. And wise guides know the effectiveness of an egg pattern fished year-round.) They then deposit a portion of their eggs into the redd, usually fifty to one hundred of the several thousand they will release. Those eggs are then fertilized by milt (or sperm) carrying males in a melee of lusty competition, with the burliest specimens often ousting lesser fish in the race to squirt first. Fertilized eggs, with developing eyes and organs, are covered in riffle and tailout habitats with well-aerated gravel free of oxygen-suffocating sediment and less prone to fungus and freeze-up.

Trout deposit eggs within a range of water depths and velocities to minimize the risk of their offspring being left high and dry due to fluctuating water levels. Adequate water depth and sediment-free spawning gravels are essential to purging spaces in the gravel, bringing oxygen to the eggs, and removing wastes associated with incubation and hatching. After hatching, young trout remain in the gravel cradle until most of their yolk reserves run out. They eventually emerge as swimming fry with their sights set on finding food to survive and thrive during the next several life phases.

Once an egg is fertilized, and depending on river temperature, it takes six to eight weeks to hatch into its alevin phase. At this stage, the young fish has hatched from the egg but remains protected within the gravel bed while it retains its egg sac and relies on the yolk for nutrition. The yolk essentially acts as an IV life-support system, supplying nutrients and energy as needed. Once the sac is entirely consumed and absorbed, the trout enters its next life phase as a free-swimming fry reliant on external sources—macroinvertebrates, algae, plankton, and soon—for nutrition.

Trout are generally considered fry during their first year of life in the river. Once fry reach 1 to 4 inches they enter what's called the fingerling stage before transforming into smolts during their second growth season. At this time trout are known as "parr" and are characterized by bars or a series of parallel vertical markings along their flanks. As smolts, juvenile fish undergo physiological, behavioral, and physical transformations, enabling them to adapt to the new environment until they shed their parr markings and take on the silvery complexions we associate with healthy adult fish.

Trout phases in a jar. From egg to alevin to fry to fingerling to adult, a rainbow trout's life is marked by distinct physical as well as behavioral characteristics.

Resident adults, like the larger browns we shocked out of the Poudre, do not leave their natal system prior to spawning. Upon maturation, they undergo additional physiological, behavioral, and physical changes to ready them for the mating ritual and to repeat the cycle. The most obvious physical changes occur in the form of color—from silver to deep and distinct spawning colors, as well as morphology. Egg-carrying females develop a distinct belly bump, while some males undergo a Frankenstein-like metamorphosis marked by kyped jaws housing jagged teeth to edge out weaker competition near the nest.

Once the male trout reaches age two to three, and females reach age three to four, their sexual maturation is mostly complete, and this in-river cycle is set to repeat. Notably, it's never an easy go. According to experts, about 90 percent of the 2,000 to 6,000 eggs wild trout deposit in the river never make it to the fry stage. Even more daunting, more than 50 percent of those fry won't survive their first year in the river—falling victim to predators from both above and below.

Adult trout can live in the river for nine-plus years and, depending on habitat and available food sources, can reach formidable sizes of 25 to 30-plus inches— especially in forage-rich tailwaters and lakes. On the Poudre, this kind of bulk is virtually unattainable due to environmental factors such as long and cold Rocky Mountain winters, which equal an abbreviated growing season. This also works to stymie any prolific and sustained hatch events. It's a rough neighborhood to grow up a trout. But here they are.

According to biologists, the Poudre is a prime example of a hatchery-propagated river, which is starting to see "promising" natural reproduction. To make things more promising, especially for the river's struggling rainbow populations, CDOW biologists, including Davies, Eric Featherman, and George Schlisler, recently instigated what's been dubbed the "brown trout removal project." Essentially—and it's not as bad as it sounds—in a series of in-river experiments, browns have been transported from one river stretch to another to provide adequate foot-hold for re-introduced hatchery rainbows in very specific habitats.

Before we delve deeper, it's important to note the genetic histories of these new, constantly evolving hybridized breeds of hatchery rainbows. As discussed earlier, when whirling disease ransacked rivers such as Montana's Madison and Colorado's Poudre, native rain-bows that had never been exposed to it suffered fatally. This is a well-documented phenomenon. When it came to finding a solution to the German-born conundrum, American biologists went back to the source. What they discovered there was that in addition to whirling disease-resistant browns, Germany also had its very own whirl-ing disease-resistant rainbow: the Hofer. Aha! Biologists speculated that if the Hofer could successfully survive in infected waters abroad, why couldn't it do the same in Colorado? The solution was simple: transplant disease-resistant Hofers into American waters and erase the mis-takes of the past with a second coming of the rainbow trout. Unfortunately, this has not been the case. Hofers, like foreign language students dumped into American schools and expected to excel in English, have mostly failed miserably in their new underwater classrooms.

According to Davies, because Hofers have been con-ditioned to survive best in hatchery scenarios "they've lost a lot of their natal instincts that would help them sur-vive in the Colorado wild. If you were to raise your hand over a hatchery raceway," he continues, "[Hofer rain-bows] rise to the surface because they see a guy coming to feed them. The fish responds because it will do better than its friends hiding on the bottom."

Although this behavior works in a hatchery setting, in the wild, when a bird of prey lifts its wings to descend on a stocker trout of subpar wit and intellect, the fish that rises to the occasion will soon find itself at the bottom of a belly. It's not the best scenario, but CDOW biologists are not ready to confiscate passports and give Hofers the boot just yet. Instead, they're currently working with hybrids, crossbreeding Hofers with Colorado River and other native rainbows in order to bolster survival instincts, while maintaining inherent anti-whirling defense mechanisms.

The crossbreed concept is a novel idea, but on the Poudre biologists continued to hit snags. This brings us back to the brown trout removal project where, starting in August 2010, biologists began shocking, bagging, and relocating brown trout from several catch-and-release sections within the Poudre canyon. By moving the browns out biologists hoped to give Hofer-crosses room to establish a foothold—before territorial browns migrated back in. The problem with the Poudre, at least from the biologists' perspective, was that wild browns had become so prolific, and occupied so much prime habitat in the system, that the new rainbows on the block were constantly outcompeted—and hence perished before they were able to spawn and join the block party.

Moreover, when browns and rainbows coexist in a river they adapt and occupy different niches. Those niches are sought based on feeding habits, or tendencies toward different modes of feeding. For example, brown trout don't necessarily want to be feeding in a riffle. Instead they often seek undercut banks and deeper pockets and holes, where their predatory, piscivorous instincts can shine. What biologists discovered on the Poudre, Davies says, "is as the brown trout population grew they would move into all niches, even those once occupied by rainbows because of competition for space—even if those spaces weren't ideal."

In order to create a more idyllic setting for introduced rainbows, as well as document the interactions between brown trout and Hofer rainbow strains, including potential for competition, predation, emigration, survival, and growth, CDOW dumped 2,000 Hofer rainbows in a 0.6-mile stretch, where browns had been removed. Six miles below, another 0.6-mile section received an additional 2,000 rainbows. In this location, however, they would swim with already present wild browns as a control. Above and below both sections, antennas were placed along the riverbed to follow the ensuing action. All rainbows and hundreds of browns above and below the sections received PIT (Passive Integrated Transponder) tags. Hundreds of browns within the control section were also tagged. When a tag passed over an antenna, it picked up the signal for that fish.

Adult browns in the Poudre River run the show. Although introduced, they have been naturally reproducing well in the wild and currently predominate over stocker rainbows by about a 60:40 split.

Initial results showed that browns moved back into the removal section fairly quickly. Within four days a significant number had navigated low water, falls, and high steps, traveling miles upstream to their former haunts. At last count the composition of the upper 0.6-mile stretch was 63 percent rainbow and 37 percent browns. In the control section, the composition was 55 percent rainbows and 45 percent browns. As we know, the historic ratio of rainbows to browns in the Poudre was 60:40. So far biologists have collected more than a million data points from fish movement. Further analysis is underway.

What does this rainbow and brown back-and-forth mean for you, the fly fisher? From a strictly fishing perspective, if you live to catch rainbows CDOW biologists certainly have your best interests in mind. Rainbows that had been decimated in systems such as the Poudre have been given a fighting chance to wage comebacks and establish a niche, with the ultimate goal of reinstating the natural reproduction cycle.

The removal project also tells us a lot about the tenacity of the competition: wild, naturally reproducing browns. Those exiled browns from the project that didn't make it back to old stomping grounds stayed put and indulged.

After their preliminary work was completed, biologists came back and sampled the river three months later to calculate growth rates, and gauge movement, survival, and health throughout the stations. As the analysis streamed in, they soon realized something was awry. All fish within the survey areas that received PIT tags had had their adipose fins clipped. But as workers began tallying results they started "beeping" more and more fish with adipose fins fully intact. Trout do not grow back adipose fins within ninety days, and at first biologists downplayed the fishy statistics as a one-time anomaly, "like maybe we missed one," Davies says. But once more of these browns began showing up in the counts a red flag was raised.

"We put the rainbows in at 7 and 8 inches. The average size of browns in that section was a little less than 14 inches," Davies adds. "We thought that a stocked rainbow at about 50 to 60 percent of the wild browns would be okay—since most predation happens on fish in the 30-percent body length."

As it turned out, many of the more aggressive browns had choked down hatchery rainbows, and what the removal project team had stumbled upon were the PIT tags of scarfed hatchery rainbows. What's more fascinating is the incomprehensible size of rainbow the browns were willing to make their lunch. The biggest meal encountered was a half-digested rainbow nearly 70 percent its host's body length. That's the equivalent of a 20-inch trout swallowing a 14-inch filet mignon. Although Davies says this predatory aspect has not been a significant detriment to the survival of these stocker rainbows, it's obvious who runs the block these days. And when it comes to feeding browns, at least in the Poudre River, don't leave rainbow patterns off the menu—especially big ones.

4 Water: The Lifeblood

Case Study: North Platte River, Wyoming, and Yellowstone River, Montana

Action and reaction, ebb and flow, trial and error, change—this is the rhythm of living.

—Bruce Barton

Graves were unmarked, fallen house timbers and corrals burned up in old campfires. Nothing much but weather and distance, the distance punctuated once in a while by ranch gates, and to the north the endless murmur and sun-flash of semis rolling along the interstate.

—Annie Proulx, *Close Range: Wyoming Stories*

In April 2011, Alcova, Wyoming—the Grey Reef gateway to the North Platte River—was still locked in harsh winter. Endless snowpack. Brimming reservoirs. Wind, always. Wayward trout from Pathfinder Reservoir dropped 40 feet over a sheer cliff and belly-flopped into Freemont Canyon . . . and the mouths of hungry pelicans. Rivers surged for longer than average. Hatches stalled, pushed forward by weeks. The North Platte's under armor was scrubbed and scoured by prolonged bouts of heavy water. Spawning habitat benefitted. Trout prospered. With no end to a marathon winter in view, spring was eventually skipped entirely. Summer arrived sometime in September. Fishing remained good through late fall.

One year later, the changes were marked. Daytime highs for April soared into the 80s. Highway snow-drifts melted to pathetic snarls of grit and dust, and we launched our drift boat at Government Bridge in shorts and T-shirts. Grey Reef guide Stu Birdsong and retired Casper-area fisheries manager Bill Wichers joined for the ride, with Wichers already talking dry flies—intent on catching a fish on a hopper before May. Year-round dry-fly fishing is an anomaly on the Grey Reef system. In 2010, there was fantastic summer terrestrial fishing. In 2011, it was dismal. This particular day saw rafts of Bae-tis on the water by midafternoon, but finding topwater feeders was an exercise in patience and, more so, dumb luck. So we spent the morning hucking nymph rigs and turning fish. When Wichers's rig anchored itself to the river bottom at day's end, he pulled hard and it returned to the boat in a mess of curled spaghetti. He immediately retired Thingamobber, clinched on a hopper, and about midway through his third cast it got gobbled. It was an oddball event for the Reef in April, the kind of fishing Wichers lives for, in a river system he helped usher from the brink of collapse to the forefront of trophy waters in the American West.

Wichers began his fisheries career soon after receiving a master's degree in fish sciences from the University of Wyoming. He followed familial footsteps; his father worked for the Fish & Wildlife Service and his grandfather was one of the first fisheries biologists in the US at the turn of the twentieth century, when the Mississippi River's commercial mussel supply collapsed in conjunction with a bustling button industry. Much of Wichers's fish know-how may have come genetically; he doesn't know, but there is no denying that his path to fly-fishing enlightenment began early. Wichers started work as a fledgling fisheries biologist at the UW's water resources research institute before departing for a Wyoming Game & Fish Department position in Buffalo, a little over a year later. In Buffalo he was met with a bevy of scum-sucking carp and was tasked to reduce their populations in Keyhole Reservoir in order to bolster its recreational fishing potential for other fish species. Netting fish was the fix du jour, but Wichers went against the grain, implementing a forage fish strategy and introducing emerald and spot tail shiners and gizzard shad to compete with carp for zooplankton, their primary food source. This unconventional—for the time—plan worked. And with victory under his belt, Wichers was on the move again. He landed in Casper in 1987, where he was about to be confronted with his most daunting fisheries challenge yet.

In April 1987, Conoco Inc. sent gallons of gasoline coursing into Bolton Creek via a ruptured pipeline. Bolton is a tributary of the North Platte near the same Government Bridge we'd started at earlier in the morning. The spill killed more than 100,000 trout from the bridge downstream, about 25 miles, to Casper. At the time, Wichers and his staff had just completed trout population estimates on the same stretch of river. "It had a devastating impact on the fishery," he says. "But while we were in the process of fixing it and building a plan for recovery, we noticed something else: sediment build-up in the system, which was dogging our recovery efforts."

Reintroduced trout, mostly rainbows and a handful of Yellowstone cutts, experienced hard times regaining their former foothold. Hatchery fish were bucketed into the system, but high sediment loads suffocated their reproduction efforts. Fine sediment wiggled its way into the cobblestone bottom, snuffing oxygen-thirsty trout eggs. Wichers recognized that action was in order. In conjunction with Al Conder, current fisheries supervisor for the Casper region, they went to work concocting a "flushing flow" study to help rid the river of this new sediment scourge. Their study was built on the premise that in naturally flowing, undammed rivers, annual freshet, or spring run-off was an essential element to fisheries health. Run-off scours a river of particulate matter, rolls rocks in its course downstream, reshapes the river contour providing vital habitat, and essentially rejuvenates the river bottom—ramping up trout-rearing productivity as well as the potential to bolster macroinvertebrate life. Much of Wyoming's North Platte system, however, did not function this way.

With major impoundments such as Pathfinder, Alcova, and Seminoe reservoirs, it had been engineered for water storage and hydroelectricity production at the dams. The trout fishery was an afterthought. But for Wichers and Conder, it remained a forefront concern. Likewise, the two young fisheries workers saw something bigger: the potential for a world-class fishery and economic driver on par with some of the best tailwater trout producers in the country. The implementation of a flushing-flow regime to simulate natural run-off and mobilize sediment downstream, off prime spawning habitat, was step one. They penned a proposal for enhanced instream flows, sent it to their superiors in Cheyenne, and worked with the Bureau of Reclamation to institute a solution.

"Since then we've been able to produce an evolved habitat component, which translates into very good spawning and excellent food producing conditions," Wichers says. "As a result we've been able to maintain a high-quality fishery from year to year, instead of the big ups and downs we used to see."

Since the Conoco spill of '87, the Platte fishery has come full circle with more pounds of trout per river mile and a higher standing crop than it has ever seen. And for a largely manmade system, one consisting of massive reservoirs and concrete impediments with fishy pinches of river sandwiched in between, the flushing-flow regime

Photo by Geoff Mueller

A Grey Reef rainbow ready for release on a blustery Wyoming winter day. This trout and its brethren can thank their size and overall health to the flushing-flow regimes implemented by area fisheries biologists Bill Wichers and Al Conder.

has provided a "natural" element of annual hope. The spring flush occurs in mid to late March on Grey Reef, before the rainbow spawn is set in motion. It starts with a base flow of 500 cfs, which is cranked up to 4,000 cfs overnight. That high flow is maintained for five or six hours before it's dropped back down to 500 cfs the following morning. In years where there is more silt than usual, fisheries management has added an early October flush, before the browns begin their spawn. "What we're trying to mimic is that cleansing you get during high spring run-off," Wichers says. "That's variable from year to year. In a natural system some years you get high run-off, some you get very little. This is a medium-type run-off, but we get it every year with consistency and it makes a hell of a difference."

On the Reef, the flush has been geared for two purposes: First, to clean gravel areas and remove fine sediment and silt, which packs into cracks like concrete and smothers trout eggs. "When you have clean gravel, you have water circulating through it ushering oxygen in that eggs need to survive and develop into juvenile trout," Wichers says. The second part of the equation is

Midge activity is prolific on the Grey Reef section of Wyoming's North Platte River.

Photo by Geoff Mueller

to replicate the same bottom-scouring result on larger rocks scattered throughout the river. These larger rocks, such as those located in runs and riffles, have the potential to produce food: mayflies, stoneflies, and caddis, for instance. "By cleaning those areas flowing past larger size rocks, those bugs have a larger surface area to exist on, to crawl underneath and inside the cracks," he adds. "If that bottom is filled with silt to the top edge of the rocks, those bugs have much less surface area to colonize and their numbers plummet."

Today the Reef teems with bug life and its trout show remarkable health—both in numbers and size. Every year Frankenfish emerge, double-digit browns and rainbows swimming the memory cards of point-and-shoots passed hand-to-hand in the dark, hushed recesses of Alcova's Sunset Grill. Sloanes General Store, across the street, sells breakfast burritos that will rock your gut, while the images of boss hogs on the wall remind you it's the fishing not the food that instigated your 4 a.m. wake-up earlier that day. With 5,000 pounds of trout per mile, Grey Reef ushers in fans from far and wide.

"Those numbers have helped develop the reputation that the river has now," Wichers says. "That combined with an increased interest in fly fishing helped by the Internet and magazines, all of that has contributed to a greater interest and knowledge base surrounding this area."

How have trout reacted to the fanfare and flotillas of boats that hammer it on a daily basis during prime season? When it comes to prime habitat and fantastic feeding events there are no complaints. Currently there is limited in-river stocking at Grey Reef, although fish are stocked in Pathfinder and Seminoe reservoirs. During high-water years, some of those trout make a jailbreak into downstream river fisheries. Of the resident fish, habitat tends to favor rainbows over browns. According to Wichers, "The quality of the spawning habitat is pretty much the same for browns and 'bows. Both species are looking at about 500 cfs. Browns have this flow almost all the way through until their eggs hatch." The difference is the upper river's faster-water, riffle-run cadence provides Golden Corral-like habitat for feasting rainbows. The river also lacks an abundance of deep holes, undercut banks, logjams, and the microhabitats where browns flourish. As far as forage fish, browns have juvenile rainbows and suckers to chew on, but little else. Regardless, there are sizable browns in the Grey reef system, and like browns anywhere else, they can be more difficult to catch.

Although brown and rainbow catching can be gang-busters on the Reef, another anomaly exists in this system that dictates how we fish, and it stems from well below the surface. Grey Reef is a place where visiting fishers typically hire guides, fish from drift boats, and crush big fish in high volumes under indicator rigs or chucking large streamers on sink-tip systems. And this all occurs amid bustling daily hatch activity: mayflies and midges in the film, on the surface, trapped in pockets and pools—with nary a happy hungry head to greet them. So what gives? Obvious red flags might include water clarity, or lack thereof. Exacerbated overhead predation. Funky water temperature fluctuations. Or hunker-down genet-ics. But according to Wichers it's likely a case of just plain laziness. In other words, Reef trout rise less frequently during some hatches because, simply, there is no need.

"Over the years I've come to the conclusion that there's so much aquatic food available, primarily insects and scuds in the river, and coming off the bottom or off the aquatic vegetation in summer, that those fish are entirely fixated there," he says.

The Reef also lacks prolific stonefly, October cad-dis, and hopper "events"—high protein meals that drive supersize fish to feed on top. Instead, much of their feed-ing opportunity exists on the river bottom and these trout like to station there, while gorging on a mixed bag of midges, micromays, scuds, and annelids. But that doesn't keep Wichers from testing and tinkering with fandangled theories, including hoppers in early April. Today Grey Reef brims with readable habitat, where fishing is often as consistent as Wyoming wind. It wouldn't be this way without trout trailblazers such as Wichers and Conder, who've made perhaps one of the world's most far-from-freestone systems of dams and impoundments a home for some supernatural trout.

Tailwater trout, such as this beauty brown from eastern Montana's Bighorn River, have adapted to take full advantage of four seasons of optimal feeding conditions.

Photo by Geoff Mueller

Tactics for Tailwater Trout

Trout have done a stellar job adapting to the idiosyncrasies of life in their artificially enhanced tailwater environments. And let's face it, despite all the conservation talk about removing them to restore migratory waterways for salmon and steelhead, bottom-release dams provide some of the best trout fishing opportunities in the country. Consistent water temps and revolving hatches through four seasons offer underwater inhabitants extended growing seasons. In a perfect world, this equals fat trout for you to target year-round. Savvy fly fishers have been taking advantage of this obesity phenomenon that—minus categorical shifts in flow regimes, or natural and unnatural occurrences of traumatic consequence—offers relatively easy-to-map guidelines for when and where to target hungry tailwater trout. For instance, we know that spring marks Baetis time for many Western tailwaters. Come early summer, stoneflies, caddis, PMDs, drakes, and other major hatch events saunter or explode into the equation. By fall, hoppers and terrestrials are tailwater go-tos, Baetis often make a second appearance, and if you like to throw meat, now's the time to brandish your streamer sticks. When nothing is popping on the surface, tailwater trout slurp scuds, annelids, eggs, caddis larva, midge pupa, and mayfly nymphs. Eating time is essentially all the time.

Tailwaters from the Delaware in New York's Catskill region to the Arkansas River below Pueblo Reservoir in Colorado each possess their own nuanced personalities. What they share in common is reliability. By understanding habitat basics, and how trout navigate these environments during specific times of the year, you can master most of them in short order. The following is a six-step primer to how.

Be in the right place at the wrong time

There's something to be said for the backward logic of being in the right place at the *wrong* time, especially when it comes to tailwaters. The best advertised fishing preached by fly shops, guides, and outfitters typically occurs during late spring through summertime during post-run-off dam releases. Although this window surely offers great fishing, particularly on dry flies, the hype also drives angler traffic to high levels. Thus, one of a tailwater's best traits is the luxury it affords you to hit timeout and wait for the angler storms to subside. Keep this in mind: No matter what time of the year, tailwater trout are constantly ready for action thanks to the dynamic nature

Brave the frostbite conditions of late, late fall on Wyoming's Miracle Mile for a shot at big browns on the swing.

of their forage rich habitats stacked with biomass—no matter how late or early you show up to the party. These trout can be found gorging on midges during balmy February afternoons on the Green River, below flaming Gorge Dam. Topwater targets are next to nil in November on the Bighorn, but the streamer fishing—and lack of boats—is something worth seeking. Shoulder season on tailwaters provides plan B and C options overlooked by the blockbuster hatch-chasing hoards. For proof, tie on a hopper in late September on Calgary's Bow River and hold on. You won't be lonely for long.

Stay in tune with the spawn

Targeting spawning trout is a surefire way to find pheromone-crazed fish in habitats replete with telltale underwater markers. See that scoured circular depression on the river bottom? Good, now cast your egg . . . and behold. This is also about as low as you can sink when it comes to sensible, ethical angling practices. But that does not mean you shouldn't be on the water during fall on the Miracle Mile, when big browns hit their annual mating grounds. Or, during spring rainbow-staging season on Montana's Madison River. Good fishing during spawning time is just a matter of knowing what habitats to avoid, and which ones produce the kind of trout that are less preoccupied with making sexual plays and releasing milt and eggs. Trout spawn in clean, oxygenated, cobblestone environments, and redds are found in long runs and shallow tailout stretches above riffles. Leave these fish undisturbed and focus your efforts elsewhere. Hit the swifter riffles, heads of runs, and bouldered pocketwater for trout hammering aquatic invertebrates, and fish bankside structure such as blow-downs and undercuts for your streamers and hopper-dropper combo rigs.

Don't overlook the skinny stuff

Tailwaters offer a wide range of trout-friendly habitat features. Riffle-run-pool scenarios. Braided side channels with a smattering of midstream boulders. Underwater vegetation for trout to suck in scuds, while staying hidden from above. And overhead bankside cover, just to name a few. Trout utilize these unique habitats during different seasons, varying times of day or night, during fluctuating temperatures ranges, and depending on when and what they're feeding on. But during low flows of late spring and summer, do not overlook the skinny stuff. Any water deep enough to house mayfly or terrestrial foraging trout is fair game. Active and oftentimes very large trout like to feed in skinny, fast, oxygenated water, especially in back eddies and along banks that move, channel, and trap insects in large quantities. These trout are looking up and call for ultrastealthy approaches because of their proximity to dry land and potential predators such as you or me. When wading, never storm into the water without first assessing the bankside situation—from a high-and-dry vantage point. Look for clues such as noses barely breaking the surface during a September trico hatch. And in clear water focus your polarized lenses on the subsurface clues, such as undulating fins, whites that become present from the chowing motion of a feeding trout's maw, and flashes that mark nymphing trout in the mid to lower water column. Once you've covered this water thoroughly, proceed to scout the river's deeper recesses. But as a rule of thumb when wading tailwaters, always source the skinny stuff first.

Leave the boat on shore

Tailwaters and drift boats go together like hash and eggs. But there's no steadfast rule saying you must float, or one that precludes you from dabbling in the pancakes at the other end of the table. Every year people drop big bucks to float with their preferred guides on famed tailwaters from East to West. And there's no doubt drift boats and rafts offer several niceties, including the ability to house a Yeti cooler brimming with ice-cold beers, or the mobility to cover large tracts of water in a relatively short amount of daylight. But walking and stalking offers advantages, too. The drift boat MO on most tailwaters involves an indicator rig built to a set length and fished within roll-casting distance of the boat. Your guide, who presumably knows where the fish lie, maneuvers the whole ensemble into range and then screams at you to "Strike!" or "Set!" or "Wake up, dumbass!" when any subsurface disturbance ensues. For some, this is mindless fishing. No arguing, it's also effective. Walking and wading, on the other hand, can provide a more cerebral experience, allowing you to get intimate with set sections of river, to glean trial-and-error beta, and to fish water more thoroughly than you would from a moving boat. If the guided float is your preference—and it's a great option for

Putting the drift boat in park on Montana's Missouri River is a great way to sleuth and target stationary sippers from shore.

river first-timers seeking a blueprint of habitats and inhabitants—don't shy from asking to stop and fish a stretch. Any professional guide worth his or her salt will have accommodating options for you to get your feet wet and see the river from a new and engaging perspective.

Break them down to size

Large tailwaters can seem intimidating at first glance. And trout habitats can be difficult to read from above. The Grey Reef, for instance, has been deemed "The Ditch" by many patrons because of its seemingly featureless nature. But don't let this deter you from finding fish. One of the first steps to tailwater success involves an accurate reading of its varied water types, and one of the most effective ways to learn these areas is by parsing large rivers into easily digestible components. Things to look for include areas that break or impede flow and provide trout places to rest and feed. Tailwater trout amass in these microhabitats that offer respite in the form of subsurface structure. Rip-rap banks are great for lurking browns looking to ambush easy prey. Islands and side channels allow you to break down a large section of river into easy-to-read, small-stream attributes. Target riffles, drop-offs, and deeper buckets where trout congregate, and fish the seams and bubble lines formed by submerged boulders and bankside deadfall. The mouths of tributary streams offer temperature variations and are another prime trout target when the main stem river heats up during summertime flows, or when trout stage during the prespawn. Large Western tailwaters, such as the South Fork of the Snake, offer these variables in abundance. The key is to not be overwhelmed by the larger picture. Focus on the smaller nuances, and you'll consistently find large trout.

Target the Pink Alberts over the Paris Hiltons

Forget salmonflies on the Henry's Fork. Green Drakes on the Frying Pan. March Browns on Silver Creek. Although the best of these hatches bring fish to the surface and are a well-worth-

it spectacle, they also drive hoards of anglers competing for limited available real estate. Instead, do yourself a favor and source a cycle spring cicada hatch. You won't see many of these sci-fi flies on the water, but when you hear that "clickity-click" broadcasted via bankside vegetation, you'll know it's game on. Similar must-hit, underfished hatches include October caddis in the West and rusty spinner falls in the East. And ants! Tailwater trout gobble a good ant hatch and you won't find the "event" on billboards as you drive through trout fishing epicenters such as Bozeman and West Yellowstone. These second-string hatches may not garner the limelight of sexier bugs we've come to know and love, but you'll often find more room to spread out and explore, and very willing fish on some of the country's most angler-overpopulated tailwater reaches.

YELLOWSTONE

Will the infant pulled at the timer's bell from a plastic womb where it has been deprived of rhythm, mother-bond, and the jostlings of everyday life not have some small space between its eyes filled with synthetic fluid, not bear, if nowhere else, in the core of its heart, the android's mark?

—Tom Robbins, *Still Life With Woodpecker*

Grey Reef owes its exceptional trouting to—among other things—the toying of flows determined by a couple of young, ambitious fisheries managers. Its brown and rainbow populations have been given life-sustaining, year-round flows in which to thrive. Fishers should be thankful to the Wicherses and Conders of the world. Montana's Yellowstone River, as far as another big swinging example of trout clout, is another book of stories. The Yellowstone, for instance, is the largest undammed river in North America and, despite encroaching development, highways and byways, and a 2011 ExxonMobil spill that temporarily sullied its downstream habitats, it flows similarly to how it did when Lewis and Clark first dipped toes in and dispatched Joseph Fields up the "Rochejaune" in April, 1805. Although home to browns, rainbows, and an assortment of other finned characters, the Yellowstone is perhaps best known for its native populations of cutthroat trout and the nuanced habitats that have afforded these fish room to roam since the get-go.

Yellowstone cutthroat (*Oncorhynchus clarki bouvieri*) of Yellowstone Lake have been the subject of intense study and conservation efforts stemming back to the '50s, when populations dived due to angling pressure and voracious dining by the birds and bruins of Yellowstone

National Park. Prior to that, tens of millions of Yellowstone cutthroat eggs were fertilized and shipped across much of the US and Canada and to countries across the globe. These cutts were (and remain) coveted for their golden hues, bejeweled black spotting, telltale crimson throat slashes, and an opportunistic reaction to feather and hook. Today they face plenty of threats on home turf, including a warming climate, habitat degradation linked to dewatering, and the explosion of nonnative lake trout in Yellowstone Lake and downstream through the river system.

Anglers swarm Yellowstone National Park annually to tangle with its namesake cutthroat trout. Kat Yarbrough hoists a beastly prize from far off the geyser-tour grid.

Photo by Geoff Mueller

58

Of those trout currently inhabiting the Yellowstone—including westslope and Yellowstone cutts, brookies, rainbows, and browns—it's the cutthroat populations that net the most press, especially when it comes to efforts aimed at preserving their esteemed legacies. The namesake subspecies is, of course, native to the system and since nonnative trout have entered the bouillabaisse over the past hundred years it's been a black-eyed ride punctuated by competition, displacement and, in some cases, near extirpation of the 'Stone's original cutts.

Fisheries biologist Brad Shepard has been ingrained in the trials of Yellowstone cutthroat over the course of a thirty-year career with Montana Fish, Wildlife & Parks. He served as both district and cutthroat conservation biologist at FWP and today works out of Livingston, Montana, as senior aquatic scientist for the Wildlife Conservation Society. His goal is to conserve and maintain the species, and it's based on a keen appreciation of the Yellowstone system, its various basins, and how trout interact and function below its unruly surface. Understanding and mapping this habitat has been key to mastering the intricacies of its quarry.

The Yellowstone, from its headwaters in YNP to where it funnels into the Missouri near Buford, North Dakota, runs approximately 678 miles. It's similar in length to the entire North Platte system and, because of that, its study presents a daunting challenge. In order to bring the 'Stone down to size, Shepard and colleagues compartmentalize the river for research purposes, focusing on specific areas and microhabitats that are later linked to the larger picture. The Shields River, for instance, is a major Yellowstone tributary that drains Montana's Crazy Mountains over a 62-mile journey that ends at its confluence just east of Livingston. The Shields represents a critical research piece to the Yellowstone cutthroat puzzle because it's mostly devoid of rainbows which, when crossbred with native cutts, muddy the genetic pool.

According to Shepard, rainbows and brook trout are a cutthroat's fiercest competition. "They are the ones that really hammer them because their distributions over-lap, leading to interbreeding and hybridization," he says. "Brook trout, on the other hand, displace cutts at higher elevations in the tributaries, but that is reversible [by way of fisheries management]. When rainbows integrate with them, there's no going back." Browns in the main stem Yellowstone also compete with and prey on cutthroat, but the two species have adapted to co-exist relatively harmoniously.

Rainbows have been historically blocked from much of the Shields via an irrigation diversion that was rebuilt with a fish ladder and trap in 2012. The barrier is located about 12 miles above the mouth and essentially provides native trout protection throughout the upstream Shields basin. From a conservation perspective, this section of the Shields provides a perfect case study. And what the river holds below the Shield's gnarled shoulders and bal-anced riffle-run-pool persona is a healthy mix of prime cutthroat habitats. Yellowstone cutthroat are essentially nonterritorial and heavily dependent on pools, where they form dominance hierarchies based on individual size and health. These trout stack in the slow moving, deeper recesses in high densities and seek clean, scrubbed gravel to spawn. Juvenile cutts use the same areas to overwinter in the cobblestones. And unlike browns, they are less dependent on debris and overhead cover, but they will cling to it, predominantly in winter.

Shields cutthroat average 10 to 14 inches. In the main stem Yellowstone they grow much larger; 16-plus-inch fish are not unusual. In Yellowstone Lake fly fishers regularly find cutts of 4 to 5 pounds. And variables that produce size are relative to the distinct habitats pre-sented from lake on downstream as the river changes geography, topography, elevation, shape, size, and tem-perature from start to finish. Unlike Wichers' Platte, with year-round nature-meets-man manipulated controls—consistent temperatures, hatches, and clockwork flows—these are basically exempt from the Yellowstone picture. But its trout have adapted accordingly, because this is the genius of a species that has thrived for millennia. According to Shepard, freestones such as the 'Stone are stochastic, or highly variable, in nature. "In some years you have floods and in some years you have drought, but the fish have figured out how to deal with that," he says.

The effects of these ups and downs directly affect Yellowstone cutts, as far as population health is concerned. High flows and idyllic water years scour the streambed, making the river more hospitable to spawning and, in turn, ratcheting up trout numbers. On the other hand, natural and unnatural events can have the opposite result. What the Yellowstone cutthroat have working in their favor is the sheer size of the Yellowstone system, undammed and free. When things go haywire in one microhabitat, native cutthroat have the luxury of marching up or downstream—in some instances upwards of 50 miles to source more hospitable staging and spawning grounds.

"This is one of the reasons that trout on the Yellowstone have developed highly migratory life histories," Shepard says. "So they can utilize the different parts of the basin for different life strategies. Cutthroat are considered 'plastic' as far as their ability to do a lot of different things. Where they have the habitat and a river population or lake population connected to tributary streams it's typical for them to move, when they have the habitat to use to their advantage."

This integral feature of the Yellowstone has been key to native cutthroat survival. When Shepard says these trout are "plastic" he's referring to these malleable life history plans and strategies. Although some Yellowstone cutts are prone to move, others may live in one pool and not saunter more than two or three riffles upstream or down to spawn—during an entire life underwater. This back-and-forth act is essentially an interplay dictated by genetic make-up in confrontation with a constantly evolving environment. One environmental factor Shepard and his colleagues continue to study is climate change. As trends on the Yellowstone point to an inevitable warm-up in decades to come, the answers they are seeking are driven by: How much? How fast? And, ultimately, how will the increased *hot* change the flow of the dwindling *sauce*?

"What we're doing is taking the climate change data and applying it to water temperatures to predict how the fish will respond," Shepard says. And, based on preliminary conclusions, so far the outlook for trout and trout fishing is not all doom and gloom. In fact, in some cases Yellowstone trout will benefit as climate change sinks in its teeth. Mid-elevation trout, for instance, would likely suffer during hot summers, but they may do better in the spring and fall with a longer growing season. At the upper end, in higher elevations, these trout are predicated to prosper, says Shepard. In the Yellowstone's lower reaches, expect the opposite. According to predictions from experts in the field, these critical temperature elements will play a lynchpin role in how native cutthroat interact with nonnative species in the future.

From a fishing perspective, it's important to note that essential temperature ranges for all trout species in the 'Stone (55° to 56°F for cutts) also coincide with choice hatch activity. During spring, those hatches include caddis, golden stones, salmon flies, March browns, and Baetis, followed by PMDs and terrestrials in summer, as well as midges, tricos, and callibaetis. Targeting river temperature, as it fluctuates with seasonal flows and the bug life it instigates, is your best barometer for finding willing fish. And Yellowstone cutthroat remain willing fly-rod targets, in some cases more so than the river's other trouty options. The adage that cutthroat are "easy" to catch is not too farfetched, according to Shepard. "I think there is some truth to that, and it's because cutthroat genetically evolved in sterile environments," he explains. "If something comes by, they are prone to check it out."

. . . .

On a grey afternoon in March 2012, Doug McKnight, Marcus McGuire, and myself backed our Clacka rig into a pre-run-off Yellowstone at the Highway 89 Bridge. The guides-day-off game plan centered on big browns— 7- and 8-weights strung for delivering filet-size flies, deep. McKnight's streamer selection is renowned beyond its Livingston roots. They are designed to strike fear in

Streamer addict and Livingston, Montana, local Doug McKnight with a nonnative, but really damn nice, brown trout.

Photo by Geoff Mueller

small fish, while provoking waylaid browns to attack. With high overcast and coolish air temps the fishing was slow. We paused on the bank to watch two horny gobblers accost a half-dozen-size harem of opportunity. We boated a handful of browns pushing 18 to 20 inches, a couple of stunned whitefish, and a rainbow and cutthroat to round out the day. Of the healthy wild mix, only two of these species were native to the Yellowstone system: One being a national treasure of sorts. The other being . . . well, a whitefish.

As far as the cutthroat's future, it's this healthy abundance of nonnatives—ones that remain coveted by guides and clients—that pose the biggest potential snag to the river's native engine. Shepard says effective Yellowstone cutthroat conservation involves "dealing" with nonnative species in order to strike a balance. "What we're promoting is that cutthroat can offer some diversity of angling opportunity," he says. "There's this feeling in the angling community that folks who want to conserve cutts also want to get rid of all the nonnative trout, and that's not the case for most of us."

Cutthroat swimming the Yellowstone's diversified waters make up a healthy 1:3 split alongside resident browns and rainbows in the river's upper reaches. Downstream of Livingston, natives have declined in recent times as spawning tribs have been hammered by drought. But catching a native cutthroat remains a reality anywhere you stand and cast well-placed flies into the system. And that is the bottom line for conservationists, such as Shepard. From freestone to tailwater, Yellowstone to North Platte and beyond, diversified waters present diversified challenges to those tasked to manage them for prosperity and posterity. Like the North Platte, good fishing is the Yellowstone's gold standard. But it's a standard that won't necessarily look the same today as it will tomorrow.

5 A Creature of Habits and Habitats

Case Study: The Blue River Stream Surgeons

On their backs were vermiculate patterns that were maps of the world in its becoming. Maps and mazes. Of a thing which could not be put back. Not be made right again. In the deep glens where they lived all things were older than man and they hummed of mystery.

—Cormac McCarthy

There's a section of the Blue River near Silverthorne, Colorado, that runs adjacent to a large white-lined lot. That swath of primo parking mostly caters to Interstate 70 passersby more interested in big-box discounts than trophy-trout fishing. But unbeknownst to the Tommy Hilfiger and GAP Outlet gawkers, this unlikely urban tailwater, located between Dillon and Green Mountain reservoirs, holds some of the largest browns and rainbows in the state. These fish swimming in a strange setting, many pushing 5-plus pounds, concentrate close to the dam, in water characterized by large boulders, pockets, deep buckets, and long, heavy runs, where they fatten up on mysis shrimp (reservoir rejects) and other macroinvertebrates inherent to the system. That prime looking river habitat, however, holding those abundant and large

Colorado's Blue River downstream of Silverthorne is a fishery that's seen its share of manmade impediments—and improvements—over the years. The author (right) and Dave Blauch of Ecological Resource Consultants enjoying the benefits of the river's revamped underwater decor.

trout, is about as naturally produced as the asphalt swath that sits next to it.

On a damp September morning in 2011, Tim Romano and I met at the Hogback park-and-ride just outside Denver. Together we jostled a pile of rod tubes and underwater camera gear into his Subaru and pointed the wheels west toward Eisenhower Tunnel. We were running late for an appointment with Dave Blauch and Troy Thompson of Ecological Resource Consultants and we were anxious to make haste as we swilled coffee and picked our way up the peaks, down the valleys, and through the fog. In addition to the caffeine intake, we were energized because this day would mark another attempt at getting into and under the water to observe trout habitat through the lens. But we were also a little worried because, at that exact moment, we were running thirty minutes late for an appointment with two engineering experts with thick credentials in hydrology and hydraulics, geomorphology, stream restoration, mine water management, and irrigation facilities—experts who could potentially cage this captive audience long enough to keep us from ever getting a cast in.

Fortunately this was not the case. After introductions and an educational stream-enhancement slideshow at ERC, Tim was soon suited up in his bright red dry suit—with a matching bright red face thanks to a too-tight gasket cinched around his neck. While Tim grappled with circulation, he stirred around in riffles and runs like a pre-spawn salmon, and every couple of minutes emerged with a new discovery to share. "You wouldn't believe it!" he said. "I just saw a 20-inch trout eat a 6-inch piece of grass! Get your ass over here and catch it!" In which case I would race over and proceed to catch nothing . . . other than sideways glares from Tim, who had by now joined team trout in laughing at my expense.

This private section of the Blue featured great riparian habitat, undercut banks, current breaking boulders, a meandering riffle-run scenario of pools and pockets, and the types of underwater decor indicative of a trout river in prime health. At first blush, it looked like a river that had been born and had remained pristine for the course of its lifetime. But that is not the case. Ironically this super section of the Blue would not have reached its current state if it weren't for the hand of man, or the scrape of the backhoe. In fact, many sections of the Blue below Silverthorne have undergone extreme stream makeovers in recent years, and one of the main architects has been Boulder-based stream restoration firm Ecological Resource Consultants (ERC). As Tim became acclimated in the stream and I peered into a fly-choked box to find a winning bug, David Blauch, the scalpel behind this particular stretch, stood upriver and threw a purposeful roll cast into the same run he helped blueprint years earlier. Blauch is originally from Pittsburgh, Pennsylvania, and has been fly fishing and analyzing trout behavior and its relation to habitat since back in his Penn State days. He graduated with a degree in Environmental Resource Management and moved to Colorado, where he ratcheted up fishing efforts and co-founded ERC based on a love for the outdoors and finding environmental solutions to keep it viable. Over the past sixteen years, Blauch has devoted much time to in-state and nationwide ecological restoration and fisheries enhancement projects, including the one we were swimming and standing in.

Over mouthfuls of bagel and our fourth round of black swill that morning, Blauch had told us, "There's a lot more to it than just throwing a rock or a log in the river. The biggest problems we see in all Western rivers are unnatural factors that have caused them to slide: water diversions or dams, flows changed from deep runs and pools to extremely wide shallow channels, and the elimination of a variety of natural habitats."

Ergo, the question inherent to ERC's work is: How do you take a river that's been pummeled by railroad and mining eras, and then had a town built on top of it, how do you take something like that and then return it to a natural system—both in terms of riparian areas and in-stream characteristics? When rivers are forced off course by channelization, flow diversions, and other adversities that develop within a watershed, the natural equilibrium or trout-sustaining balance goes awry. Many of these challenges are a direct result of development. Historically, when populations spiked and cities and new roads spawned to shoulder the load, rivers that sat in the path hit ecological rock bottom. In recent times rivers have become depositories for wastewater and raw sewage. They have been dammed, dredged, re-channelized, and tweaked to meet the needs of industrialization and commerce. And they have had their courses altered, and altered again, to better suit the demands of progress. In turn, once healthy trout populations, not to mention steelhead and salmon stocks, have been forced out, to estuaries and headwaters, and in worst-case scenarios they have been entirely extirpated from the picture.

The Blue River through Silverthorne is a product of similar variables. But its fishery—thanks to the addition of a dam and the subsequent trout-friendly tailwater effects of stabilized flows and temperatures and reasonable bug life (which is today dwindling)—has not yet been one of the casualties. Before ERC arrived on the scene the Blue already held coveted Gold Medal status from the Colorado Wildlife Commission because of its great fishing reputation. Currently less than 200 miles of Colorado's 9,000 miles of trout streams carry this distinction.

Regardless of the accolades, something was still distressing on the Blue. The river, even for all its pig trout per mile, didn't quite look or behave naturally. ERC was sought by the Town of Silverthorne to engage in the Blue River Enhancement Project—a two-phased assignment designed to ensure that the Blue River remained a prominent recreational angling attraction by restoring and enhancing its corridor to retain its status as a high-quality trout fishery. Phase I took place in 2003 and began 300 feet downstream of Interstate 70, extending south approximately 3,150 feet to the base of Dillon Dam. The 2005 Phase II project called for the enhancement of 3,735 linear feet (0.71 mile), approximately 2 miles farther downstream.

The goal was to fortify the river with habitat upgrades and combat issues stemming from reduced stream flows due to increased diversions to Colorado's Front Range and decreased trout holding capacity elevated by Colorado's homicidally cold winters. ERC's challenge was to build a river blueprint that not only promoted fish health, but would also allow elbowroom for more fishers. The idyllic typification of a Rocky Mountain trout stream is one that possesses both solitude and fish in abundance. But with the Blue sitting next to one of Colorado's more infamous east-west mountain corridors—Interstate 70—the river, just like the road, needed carrying capacity: 1) to get more people out recreating, and 2) to help drive tourism dollars toward local businesses, including two fly shops that currently occupy real-estate within walking distance of the river. And why not? The more important question for ERC, however, was: How?

· ·

From a trout's perspective a river is essentially its four-season home: where it fosters family and makes its bed; its dinner table, where it loads its plate; its commute, where it seasonally migrates between activity, rest, and cover; and its livelihood, where the bottom line is survival. In order for this home to be healthy and prosperous, many variables come into play. Trout need a steady supply of cool, clean, and oxygenated water; river architecture that supports a variety of aquatic life; and in-stream structure capable of mitigating seasonal spikes in flows, including the transport of heavy water and sediment loads during spring freshet. In addition, the most coveted trout homes in the country—think Slough Creek deep in Yellowstone National Park, or Montana's powerhouse Yellowstone River (one of the longest undammed rivers in the world)—are ones that flow how nature intended them to from the outset. These lynchpin elements to health and prosperity are formed by the forces of hydrology, geology, and topography, which are the building blocks for stream alignment, gradient, and equilibrium. When this equilibrium teeters or collapses, a trout's neighborhood becomes unkempt and dilapidated. But instead of riots in the riffles and trout turning their pectoral fins toward seedy dive-bars, they just start disappearing.

The comforts of home. Trout need a steady supply of cool, clean, oxygenated water and instream architecture that supports a variety of aquatic food sources.

According to the US Fish & Wildlife Service (USFW), which outlines ideal habitats for all trout species, the equation is even more complex. Rainbow trout (*Oncorhynchus mykiss*), for instance, live in riffles and pools, in and around submerged trees, boulders, under-cut banks, aquatic vegetation, and require the ability to "swim to and from different habitats from ocean to headwaters, or from tributary confluence to headwaters," increasing the value of these habitat components. Moreover, "Assuring fish passage through artificial barriers in a system of connected habitats greatly enhances the capability of an aquatic system to sustain rainbow trout populations."

This also rings true for other species of trout. And reading through USFW's detailed descriptions for cut-throat, brook, brown, and bull trout, much of the above rhetoric is reiterated. There are characteristics that are uniform for trout species across the spectrum, such as cool, clear water—untainted by pollutants. "There's really not a huge variety here," Blauch says. "Especially in the West. For the most part a trout, is a trout, is a trout." Similarly, for much of ERC's habitat work in Colorado, the considerations are less species specific and more in tune with a particular river environment or esthetic in its natural, historical context.

When examining a river such as the Blue, for example, an initial assessment is made regarding its current habitat—what's working versus what's not—in relation to stream type. From this snapshot Blauch and Thompson build a framework for optimization. If riparian habitat is degraded, adversely affecting hatches, riverside stability, and opportunities for cover and shade, ERC implements a reintroduction strategy—in some cases rebuilding a river from the bedrock up. In other cases, where bottom substrates have been cemented together over time and channelization has systematically eliminated good forage and trout-holding habitat, river bottoms are reassembled, and the river's path re-contoured so trout, in turn, can reestablish a foothold.

According to Thompson, "What you'll see in nature is this sinuosity: a riffle that's in a straightaway that leads into a pool. So we're always trying to replicate these riffle-pool, riffle-bend scenarios. Trout populate nearly all Western streams and rivers, but without clean water, optimum substrate and sediment loads, and proper flow conveyances, the number of trout in a given stream system will be limited."

· ·

In line with ERC's river enhancement work, bringing trout to the fold is one consideration, but another equally daunting task is building habitats that fit the mold of the fly fisher's vision. Blauch explains: "There are certain projects, on certain streams, where we're just trying to set up for the ideal drifts. In low flow you want perfect pocketwater. In extremely high flows, a lot of private groups are looking for very specific types of fishing. But the basic channel shaping and forming, that's not as much from a fly-fishing standpoint as it is creating the holding capacity, flow dynamics, and depth."

If you build it correctly the hope is that "they will come." But achieving that vision ultimately takes finesse work, which on the Blue meant manicuring a system for fishery health, as well as enhanced angler experience. When savvy fly fishers step into a river, we are looking at boulder placement, river segments where we can achieve long drifts through prime holding water, pockets, buckets, and drop-offs for nymphing, long runs for drag-free-dry-fly drifts, and places where we can execute the casts needed to best deliver our flies. Creating and re-creating these scenarios time and time again has helped bolster Blauch's growth as an effective fly fisher.

"You are really able to translate it into knowing where fish move, when they move into these pockets, and how they utilize the things you are making. You really start to see that," he says. "From a fishing perspective, you've got to take in the greater picture. Is it slackwater and all the fish are spooky and hanging off the banks? Are they nosing up in the riffles? Where are the bugs moving? These are all things you must consider."

One of the biggest surprises Blauch has experienced throughout his stream enhancement work is just how tolerant trout are to human presence—on and in the river. Most resident fish don't migrate or move very

In restored sections of Colorado's Blue River, boulders, such as the one seen here, have been strategically placed to provide ideal habitat for trout. Familiarizing yourself with the river bottom, and how trout use it, provides a blueprint for best results.

far, if they don't have to, he says. During strong spring run-off is the exception to the rule, when fish are more prone to occupying isolated pockets. After they are disturbed, whether it's an intruding fly fisher, bird of prey, or backhoe, they often move right back to their preferred lies.

As to whether or not a "manmade" or stream-enhanced section of river can ever outperform nature's natural plan, there's really little question: "An undisturbed, natural environment is the best you're ever going to do. When you get into a situation without influences from highways, railroads, mines, water diversions, and completely unnatural conditions . . . it's going to function the best," Blauch says. "In a sense of can we do better than nature? It's very hard. I think what you can do is vastly improve the state of how things are now. But a lot of the general public does not realize how impacted these streams are."

. . . .

Back on the new and enhanced Blue, feet firmly planted in our contemporary world of fishing, the river actually looks and feels surprisingly natural—much thanks to these rehabilitation efforts. The fish behave accordingly, and without much of a hatch to match, snub our flies until it's time to pack up the underwater housing, reload Tim's Subaru, battle Interstate 70, and head home. Considering the work that went into building the day's experience, it's easy to lose sight of just how far the natural world has shifted—to the point of being completely lost in many cases. Across the West there are few streams left that haven't been sucked for irrigation or impacted by the push of development. The trout, with thousands of years of instinct ingrained in those almond-size brains, however, continue to adapt.

Interpreting River Speak

The riffle. Underwater, riffles represent a microcosm of great trout habitat. They are shallow, offer a moderate to fast pace, and are heavily oxygenated due to a proliferation of static structure in the form of rocks, boulders, and some surprisingly cavernous pockets located in and around them. This gurgling, broken water offers great holding and feeding lanes for trout due to intricate currents forced to pinball downstream through an underwater maze of protruding objects. Riffles are prime launch pads for insects such as mayflies, stoneflies, and caddis. Look for trout moving from their deeper lies into riffles during peak hatch opportunities.

The run. Between the riffle and the pool lies the run. Underwater, the run offers more overhead cover for trout (and intrepid snorkelers) in the form of increasing depth and a steady, slower pace due to a lower gradient and a widening of the river topography. Water in the run can be darker due to this added depth and, depending on clarity, you may or may not be able to see bottom from above. Runs show an even-keeled pace on the surface and relatively smooth, undisturbed current lanes. They are also another prime feeding lie where, depending on the phase of the hatch, trout will occupy various levels in the water column. During nonhatch times

Good habitat is everything to a trout, and the riffle is one of its favorites. Riffles provide the right mix of structure, gradient, oxygen-rich water, and prime food sources such as mayflies, stoneflies, and caddis.

slower, deeper runs are also favorites for swinging streamers. With a switch or a small Spey rod, you can cover a ton of water here, as well as depths, by varying your sink-tip systems.

The plunge pool. Underwater, the plunge pool, located at the head of a run, looks like a swirling vortex of whitewater, with dark, bouldered recesses that offer large trout respite from heavier water located higher in the water column, closer to the river surface, as well as from the push of shallow, faster water located just upstream. From above, plunge pools are often marked by waterfalls or can be found below heavy rapids created by steep gradient or where topography forces a "pinch" in the river's course. The plunge is essentially where the water drops and pools out and can be considered the crux of where the river goes from shallow to immediately deep, initiating the head of a pool. Plunge pools are prime lies for targeting large trout, especially migratory fish that will rest at the head before working their way farther upstream through runs and riffles.

The pool. Underwater, the pool marks the deepest, slowest moving segment of a river section. In many rivers in the West, you'll find sediment buildup here and less in the way of prime structure and habitat. From above, pools can be found below the riffle and plunge, where the river widens before condensing again into the flat and tailout sections. Depending on the size and structure of the pool it can appear much like a still water, and in many instances eddies can form on either side of the main current. Although trout frequent pools, their feeding behavior here is often erratic and sporadic.

The flat. Like the name implies, flats are relatively smooth, nondescript river sections that, from underwater, are well lit from above due to a girthy midsection and minimal overhead cover. Trout can be found in flats, typically small ones. But larger fish will move in during nonfeeding or resting phases, or at night, when they're freer to roam in search of high protein items . . . like a mouse that's lost its bearings.

The tailout. Tailouts mark the tail end of the pool, where the flat begins to constrict and the top of the downstream riffle is forming below it. From underwater, the tailout can produce a divot where water stacks before it funnels and quickens pace into a gradient drop. With sediment located at the head of the pool, tailout bottoms are comparatively clean. Scoured cobblestone is often deposited here, making tailouts prime areas for spawning, as well as for resting fish. In the spring and fall, give rainbows and browns a break and avoid deliberately fishing over redds. During nonspawn times, I won't exit a run before at least swinging a couple of flies through the tailout section. Adult mayflies, tricos, caddis, and midges also move through these sections during good hatches. Keep your eyes peeled for staging sippers and rising heads.

The anomalies. Although rivers can be generally parsed into fairly standard sections, it's important to note that: 1) No river is the same, and 2) You'll catch more fish by paying attention to the subtle nuances and anomalies as opposed to focusing all your time on the blatant and basic. You'll also run into less competition by avoiding your local GPS-linked "Meat Hole." Sure, I've spent plenty of time attempting to plunge a fish or two from the Frying Pan's Toilet Bowl stretch, but I always find more rewarding fishing in the downstream sections less beat to death by the parking lot hordes.

The Frying Pan is a great example of a river that has piles of swagger when it comes to trout-friendly features and year-round hatches. There are manmade, Disney-like areas replete with multitier, cascading waterfalls that stretch from one edge of the river to the other. There's a road that runs past most of it, making access a cinch . . . as long as flows remain below the 800 cfs flood stages. There are riffles, runs, pools, flats, and tailouts, of course, but there are also subtle quirks that fish really well throughout four seasons on this healthy tailwater. These characteristics are worth keeping your eyes peeled for.

Undercut bank. In addition to the Pan, undercut banks exist on almost every river in the Western United States and they make for excellent trout hideouts. From underwater, they are dark, cavernous and on areas of the Big Thompson River in Rocky Mountain National Park, they can run more than a rod's length horizontally under your feet. A soft approach is key in such instances. Undercuts are also great places to target predatory trout with streamers, as large browns will hunker in the dark recesses, waiting to ambush an errant minnow or a well-placed Bugger. During summer and early fall, fishing terrestrials along the banks of Montana's Yellowstone River is a go-to method for covering long drifts from a boat and enticing crushing dry-fly takes. Big browns and 'bows relish the feeding lanes banks create, which concentrate hatched or hatching flies into uniform highways of easy pickins'. Whether you're slapping

An undercut lie from in looking out offers a unique fish-first perspective. These ambush zones provide prime habitat for large, lurking browns waiting to smash smaller prey.

streamers or parachuting drys, don't ignore the undercuts.

In-stream boulder or succession of boulders. Most river bottoms are a mishmash of rocks and boulders of varying shapes and sizes deposited and spaced out at varying intervals. Although nature's rhyme and reason can be difficult to decipher, sometimes its symmetry is so genius that trout cannot avoid it. Neither should you. Trout, being opportunistic, cling to areas that effectively break the tension of heavy current, alleviating the push against their streamlined bodies. These current breaks allow trout to hold, while expending less energy in search of their next meal. In-stream boulders work to the fly fisher's advantage on two

In-stream boulders are essential elements of a river's underwater landscape, providing current breaks and reprieve from faster water. Note where the water crashes at the head of the boulder, creating holding lies in the "pillows" before and aft of the obstruction.

levels: 1) they provide reprieve for trout and obvious lies for us to fish, and 2) when current pushes around these in-stream obtrusions it forces hatched and hatching insects down a one-way street where trout will line up and feed, and you can stand back, cast, and drift a fly into their path.

Above rock pocket/pillow. Although we're often told to target the prime lie (or lies) directly below rocks, do not overlook the one above or in front. Big fish will hold in this position because it offers first dibs at incoming food, as well as a sanctuary and an easy escape route from predators. From underwater looking up, water that strikes a rock pile in front of it creates a calm slot called a pillow. Trout can hold here out of the faster currents both above and to river-right and -left of the pillow. Consistently, I've hooked big Miracle Mile brown trout out of this less obvious lie, whether swinging wet flies or drifting nymphs.

Seams. Think of a river seam like a hemline on your favorite pair of pants. They form where two opposing objects meet. Like fabric, river seams produce a relatively obvious line you can see with the naked eye. Seams are formed in the river, when varying current speeds combine to create a visual line in the river's surface. Underwater, they are typically created below in-stream structure such as a large boulder or a downed tree. They are also created by varying depths of water, for instance, where a shallow bar, shoal, or shelf meets or lies adjacent to a drop. The "lift" in the river bottom will effectively slow the water, and cause a single current to split and course around it. These underwater nuances will show on the surface as the seam. The most important thing to know about seams is that they hold fish. Fish prefer seams because they provide instances where fast water meets slower water: Where a fish can hold in the slow seam, and dip into the fast seam to attack floundering prey, or mayflies and other insects that get caught up in the adhesion between two competing speeds of current. Seams essentially create feeding lanes and effective fly fishers know they are productive spots to run a nymph rig, or to position a broadside wet-fly presentation through.

Eddies. Not to be confused with "Cousin Eddy" from National Lampoon's *Vacation* series, eddies have been targeted by bait, spin, and fly chuckers since man first picked up a rod and set his mind on skinning a trout for dinner. Underwater, eddies can be found downstream of an obstruction such as a point bar that snags a corner of the river and sends it spiraling back upstream. Inside the eddy, the downstream movement of water is partially or fully arrested. Outside the eddy is typically a seam and a return to the river flowing in its natural downstream direction. Eddies exist on rivers of all shapes and sizes. Some of the most productive I've fished occur on the booming British Columbia reaches of the upper Columbia River—which can flow at 15,000 cfs or more. During the midsummer months, caddis swarm the river en masse and eventually become trapped and concentrated in massive eddies the size of supermarket parking lots and up to 20 or 30 feet deep. Because these eddies hold bugs in abundance, they are also loaded with surface-feeding trout during good hatch conditions. The trickiest thing about fishing eddies is deciphering which direction the current is moving, which direction the trout are facing and feeding, and then timing and placing your fly perfectly in the feeding lane. In larger rivers, eddies can provide dizzying dry-fly fishing—from caddis, to tricos, to PMDs to Baetis, and more.

The blowdown. Whether they are the result of an industrious beaver or a vicious wind-pummeling, trees, root wads, or any other riparian anomaly that enters the river and stays long enough to make a lasting impression on its hydraulics typically becomes a boomtown for trout—just make sure to avoid the burlier ones with your raft. Underwater, sweeping blowdowns are dark and ominous. They provide trout with the safety and security of excellent overhead cover and they stymie flows enough to offer reprieve from heavier currents. Downstream of the blowdown you'll find seams and glassy currents, where trout station to gobble bugs. Rafting Wyoming's Encampment River can be like a blowdown bumper car rally. After spring run-off and with each new season, it seems like there is a new tree to dodge around every turn from boat launch to where it meets the North Platte River above Saratoga. These blowdowns create deep buckets and shadowy habitat for big browns that lurk near the bottom, amid the inevitable snags. Be sure to bring extra bugs, and hope to ditch your Thingamabobbers for Green Drake drys come midafternoon in July.

When a tree falls down in the river . . . Downed riparian habitat that enters the river and stays long enough to make a lasting impression can become a boomtown for trout of all sizes—as well as a graveyard for errant flies.

6 What Trout See

Shades of Grey and the Great Purple
Worm Debate

When it comes to what trout see, a great place to gain a sense of perspective is your local Western lake. Stillwaters provide the fly fisher with an excellent case study for experimentation purposes. They are often clear, offer various types of underwater habitat—from submerged deadfall to shallow flats, underwater springs, and drop-offs—and they come with hatch-matching opportunities, including caddis, mayflies, damsels, scuds, chironomids/midges, and more. Stillwaters at their best also give trout an extended opportunity to inspect, snub, or devour your offerings, compared to a river where fast-moving hydraulics significantly diminish a trout's window to stop and mull it over.

After the spring melee subsides on trafficked lakes such as BC's Roche, Montana's Hebgen, or Colorado's Delaney Buttes chain, new factors enter the mix that affect how we think about trout. By July and August long, hot days lead to rising water temperatures, depleting oxygen levels, and fish that are harder to locate—hunkering down in the deepest recesses. Dropping your fly in front of more fish is the challenge, and what trout see when it comes to your fly is the changing variable.

How trout see color, whether you fish tailwaters, freestones, lakes, or beaver ponds is a vital component to the catching equation. Practice, as well as science, tells us that fish can discern color. And we know that colors of the spectrum disappear depending on their wavelength,

Colorado's Rocky Mountain National Park is rife with high-alpine stillwaters both on and off the beaten trail. This summertime view from Spruce Lake is one shared by a healthy population of prowling cutts.

as well as other variables such as water quality, clarity, and color. In stillwaters, depth can also either strip or bolster the effects of color. Imagine that light is only penetrating down about 25 feet at best on a clear lake; below that any fly pattern will be reduced to shades of grey. Ergo, below 25 feet, or on turbid, off-color rivers where opportunities for light to penetrate the water column diminish, the focus switches to size, shape, and how the fly is fished.

"But if you come into 8 feet of water in a very clear lake, why are trout so picky on color and even rib? We don't know exactly what trout are seeing but obviously if one color is working and one isn't, then they are seeing something that looks more real to them," says Brian

Chan. According to Robert J. Behnke, trout and salmon both see colors: "The cones located in the retina are sensitive to wavelengths associated with ultraviolet, blue, green, and red light. Their perception is greatest toward the blue end of the spectrum."

Chartreuse. Muted olive. Peacock. Cream. Dun. Rust. Wine. Yellow. Pearlescent. And so on. Fly fishers have experimented with more color variations than thirteen year olds at the nail polish counter debating the merits of Politely Pink vs. Insanely Indigo. Any fly shop owner worth his/her weight in #12 Pheasant Tails knows color attracts fishers to fly bins. But more than that, the right color or color combinations also lure more trout to hand. Lately, an increasing number of Rocky Mountain trout have tasted more and more blues and purples, and Behnke's blue-end-of-the-spectrum deductions about what trout see are playing true in the field. Much like humans targeting McDonald's drive-thrus during hopping holiday weekends, trout are also opportunistic feeders. In the underwater highway, whether it's caddisflies, mayflies, stoneflies, damsels, terrestrials, or a proliferation of crawfish, generally if it's in plain sight and available in abundance, it's what's for dinner. But as far as this author can tell, purple sparkle worms are next to nil in nature. The same can be said for purple Prince Nymphs and blue Copper Johns. But trout still eat them . . . all.

In our river trials, purple was plunked prolifically across northern Colorado and central Wyoming with varying results. On some systems purple crushed the competition: tailwaters such as Wyoming's North Platte and Wind rivers in particular. At the Yampa on a snowy pre-Thanksgiving weekend and on Utah's Green River, it flat out stunk—most of the time. In Kirk Deeter and Charlie Meyers's *The Little Red Book of Fly Fishing,* the authors surmise that purple catches a trout's attention better than other colors, but mainly during nonhatch conditions.

North Platte Lodge/Reef Fly Shop guide Stu Bird-song, who is well-versed in the ways of the worm—con-sidering his clients hook hundreds of Grey Reef browns and 'bows with it annually—has experimented with pur-ple extensively, pitting it against chartreuse, pink, tra-ditional red, and even brown tones closely resembling natural earthworms. His results from the high-water sea-sons of 2010 and 2011 are telling. Birdsong says, "We would throw a purple and a red simultaneously and most of the time, no matter what the color combinations, you were best off fishing two purple worms. The first couple of weeks of spring," he adds, "it was a pretty good split—trout seemed to eat the purple more, but they would eat other colors. As the season progressed and those fish

It ain't pretty to you or me, but the purple worm oozes appeal when it comes to seducing big trout on the Grey Reef.

saw more and more worm patterns, purple continued to produce over and above red, pink, or chartreuse."

In fact, purple fished so well for his clients that Birdsong and fellow Reef guide Seth Kapust stopped fishing the alternatives altogether. Birdsong says that purple's success on the North Platte is in large part due to water clarity: "I think it shows better because of the increased sediment load during high-water years, so it has a little more of what we call 'stage presence,'" he says. "If you took purple patterns to the Green River below Flaming Gorge Dam, which is amazingly clear, those patterns are going to fish differently. When purple is viewed against brown or tannin water, I think it takes on a more natural color, but one that sticks out better than other colors."

The idea that purple takes on a more "natural" color underwater is a notable observation. What we see, or perceive to see, underwater is completely different than what trout do. Take for example caddisflies. If we examine a caddis natural that appears green, it's because we're seeing the reflections of blues and yellows. If trout are seeing infrared coming off that, it's going to be a color we can't even begin to discern. The same argument can easily be made for the success of purple: trout are seeing something that we fly fishers are not. Unlike trout, the human eye is incapable of processing infrared, or ultraviolet for that matter. Perhaps there is more infrared coming off deep purples because it's a closer representation than other colors. Infrared, however, only penetrates the very top of the water column. Ultraviolet, on the other hand, will pierce much deeper—down to 300 feet or more in crystal-clear scenarios.

Lately, Brian Chan has been experimenting with UV head cements and lacquering his chironomid and midge patterns, which gives flies a purple tinge under natural light. So far his results have been inconclusive. What we do know is that reflective materials work: holographic Flashabous and other light-gathering synthetics. The key is imitating the natural in shape, form, and action as closely as possible, while at the same time adopting colors that stand out in a crowd. The Royal Wulff, for instance, provides a standard mayfly silhouette on the water's surface, but it bends the status quo with its regal peacock herl and bright white wing. These colors do not necessarily mimic a natural mayfly but they unquestionably trigger a response. The same goes for sparkle-back nymphs or the addition of gold, silver, or copper tinsel to an Intruder-type steelhead fly. These embellishments and color modifications catch fish because they stand out more readily to the trout's eye—the same way dark colors fished in dark conditions enhance silhouette and contrast.

The trout's eye is fine-tuned for spotting food and avoiding potential trouble from most angles. The combination of monocular and binocular vision allows this cutthroat to capture and process data from in front, as well as on both flanks.

Trout have a great range of vision, which can be an advantage as well as a detriment in the quest for catching more. In other words, we want trout to recognize our flies, but not us via our riverbank fumblings, and piss-poor presentations. Trout have both monocular and binocular vision. That is, trout can see objects directly in front of them with both eyes (binocular vision), as well as anything on either side of them (monocular vision). Objects directly behind the fish fall into a blind-spot of approximately 30 degrees. When trout see the silhouette of a wader-clad monster waving a 9-foot fly rod, or anything above the water surface for that matter—osprey, eagles, insects, rodents, and soon—that picture is either distorted or enhanced by refraction. Refraction is based on Snell's Law—full of "vector forms" and other nonfishy mathematical mumbo-jumbo. But what you should take home from Snell's is that it occurs when light waves are deflected at the intercept where water meets air. The result is a compression of the trout's field of vision into a cone or window that widens depending on how close a trout sits to the surface, or shrinks depending on how deep it dwells in the water. Logically, the fish can fathom more of the above water world the closer it is to the surface than it does milling around down deep.

Moreover, refraction can be thought of in terms of "Objects in the mirror are *slightly* closer than they appear," while objects located outside this cone of vision appear compressed and fuzzy. When you approach trout, keep in mind that you are a big and scary predator, one that exponentially increases in size and speed the closer you get to the fish. Thus, it pays to be low, stealthy, and methodical in your approach.

. . . .

In addition to spending countless hours head above water, casting from a jon boat or with wading boots firmly planted in one of North America's top producing lakes or

Stillwaters present deep mysteries to the untrained eye. When using strike indicators to reach set depths, be prepared to set the hook at the slightest disturbances.

rivers, Chan has on occasion peered below. Using Aqua-Vu cameras in stillwaters allows him to see how trout react to flies under an indicator, and the results speak volumes: "Oftentimes, we'll see groups of three, four, or five trout come in and look at the fly, do donuts around it, then suddenly one of those fish will break from the pack and grab it—the most aggressive one," Chan says.

On an annual June outing, Chan and his fishing partner anchored their boat in a terrace-shoaled Yukon stillwater famous for its massive chironomid hatches in shallow water over a marl bottom. There they observed lake trout up to 10 and 12 pounds and whitefish in the 5- to 7-pound class circle their pupa patterns. "They'd swim away and come back and look at it, the same fish each time," Chan says. "All of a sudden they'd swim away and one would do an abrupt 180 and beat the hell out of the fly. This is after they probably looked at it a dozen times."

Even more incredible, both the lake and whitefish encountered consistently sampled the fly, and then spit it, without ever moving the strike indicator. Their flies were dangling 8 feet deep below the surface. But no dimple. No quiver. Nothing. This observation does not bode well for the river fisher, especially considering this lake was flat calm, whereas a river is rife with riffles and other surface disturbances that make detecting unnatural movement against your strike indicator that much more difficult. In a river trout are forced to make split decisions. Oftentimes these takes go undetected and opportunities are lost. In river scenarios, one- or two-fly nymph rigs under a strike indicator are limiting, especially when it comes to what you can't see subsurface. This is either good reason to throw away your strike indicators altogether and become dry-fly purists, or promptly drive to your nearest fly shop and ask what they offer in the way of a Czech-nymphing curriculum. The latter involves enhancing your underwater fish intuition, and setting the hook at least once with every cast through the run. In other words, second-guess less, and set, set, set.

. . . .

TIPPETS—STRIKE INDICATORS AND SPLIT-SHOT

Targeting hatches is your best-case scenario for finding willing fish in numbers. These prolific bug events also afford great opportunities to test gear theories on the water. The best of these trout food supermarkets carry wide varieties of aquatic life: shopping isles of nuanced habitats brimming with terrestrials, mayflies such as

Baetis, PMDs, and drakes; caddis; salad-like vegetation crawling with scuds, daphnia, plankton; and meat departments spewing stoneflies, crawdads, sculpins, and other baitfish that hungry browns and rainbows can't resist. With steady, hatch-inducing flows of cool, clear water through four seasons, eastern Montana's Bighorn River is a tailwater example of Walmart carrying capacity. And like the big blue box store, the Bighorn is also one of the most frequented one-stop shops in the Lower 48 for fly fishers intent on finding food source selection.

The Bighorn enters Montana via Wyoming at Bighorn Reservoir. More than 90 miles later it meets the Yellowstone River, near Custer. The first 14 miles of moving water below After Bay Dam are the most heavily trafficked—and for good reason. This section of wide-open, classic Western river represents some of the best trout water in Montana, with fish counts for the upper 13 miles—from After Bay downstream to Bighorn access—topping charts at approximately 5,500 "catchables" per mile. Bighorn trout populations consist of a rainbow and brown mix. This ratio fluctuates annually, with rainbows predominating 3:1 in recent years.

In the spring of 2010, I returned to the river after a multi-year hiatus. When the flotillas of guide-propelled drift boats were clocking out for the day, we clocked in with our Clackacraft. At noon the Baetis switch turned on and bugs hatched en masse, while large trout slashed shallow riffles, gorged in the buckets and river pockets, and then retreated to the slower slicks and deeper holes to kick back and belch until it was time to pedal forward and rejoin the action.

The mayflies and accompanying midges were small. We fished #20 to 22 CDC Smoke Jumpers and Quigley Cripples on top, while experimenting with Craven's JuJubaetis as well as RS2s, Zebra Midges, and other midge variations dropped below drys. This wasn't as much of a technical hatch-matching scenario characterized by fish

Photo by Kat Yarbrough

As far as four-season fishing laboratories are concerned, it doesn't get much better than eastern Montana's Bighorn River. Hatches pop, fish are prolific, and there is no shortage of good water to test theories through trial and error.

sipping selectively. Good casts and drifts were rewarded. But fly imitations also had competition with the many naturals descending seams and blown into back eddies. The catching was, at best, sporadic. Conventional wisdom, as well as the wisdom contained within my boat and chattering at my ear, tells you that when you're missing fish the right thing to do in addition to changing flies is to regroup and decrease your tippet diameter. But for several reasons, which I'll explain more in-depth, I shunned that advice—successfully. After tallying scores with the other able casters on the water that night, it didn't hurt results.

I'm a firm believer in 4X fluorocarbon tippet because in most situations, sticking with the biggest tippet diameter you can stuff through a hook-eye beats going small for the sake of going small. To rehash what we know from underwater looking up, trout have sharp vision and keen ingrained instincts when it comes to what they do and don't want to see. Trout are also opportunistic and as long as they remain happy, they will continue to eat. Being a covert fly fisher is easier said than done. And there are many ways to tip off trout: from our approach into the river to the techniques and tackle selected to feed unassuming trout. All of these elements are interconnected on the water. Presentation, however—or more specifically our delivery of the fly—is paramount to this multi-tiered equation. Good presentation often trumps a skinnier strand of tippet, and in order to comprehend this it helps to understand your fluoros and monos from a trout's-eye view. No person on—or in—the river knows this better than perhaps Ralph Cutter of the California School of Fly Fishing. Cutter, who established his school in 1981, has spent an extensive portion of his career underwater with trout, incorporating the lessons he's gleaned from those experiences into his curriculum. Some of Cutter's most pertinent revelations revolve around tippet, which he assures students trout see, no matter how miniscule. "A trout can see 7X tippet as well as it can see climbing rope," he says. "The flash of 7X is brilliant underwater. They may or may not see the individual strand of fiber, but they definitely see that flash and that's where fish scare."

And what about fluorocarbon tippets being less flashy than monofilaments of similar break strengths and diameters underwater? Really, it's all the same. Fluorocarbon differs from mono on several levels: it sinks more readily for one, which is why it's preferred for nymphing, throwing streamers, and other subsurface presentations. It's also less susceptible to nicks and other wear and tear, and it takes longer to break down than mono under normal environmental conditions. It is not, however, more *stealthy*. Like Cutter, we have experimented with both fluoros and monos underwater. The visual differences are nominal at best. Cutter says, "Very often the fish will be taking minute items such as daphnia or copepods that are impossible for me to see much more than a foot away. These fish routinely initiate their rise to the food when it is still 5 or 6 feet away. At that distance even I can clearly see 7X tippet, and have no doubt trout see it too.

"I don't get the debate," he adds. But it's like anything you have faith in, like a favorite fly, the more you have trust in it, the more you fish it, the more you're going to catch."

With that in mind, the mono vs. fluoro debate is essentially a human one—not a trout one—and as far as we're concerned, the trout don't care. RIO, fine makers of fly lines and tippets, advertises its spools 5X Powerflex tippet as being rated for a break-strength of 5 pounds, and coming in at a noodly .006-inch diameter. In comparison, RIO 4X Powerflex jumps to an extra pound and a half in break-strength, while sacrificing little in the way of increased diameter. A 0.001-inch bump, to be exact. But what does this mean to a trout—one that may or may not see it in the water?

Smaller tippets do not offer much benefit when it comes to hiding it from a trout. But they do offer advantages when it comes to presentation. A longer, smaller-diameter tippet can give you a subtler delivery when fishing dries—less splash and more freedom for your imitations to move "naturally" in microcurrents on the river's surface. Underwater, the same bodes true: the lighter and longer the tippet, the more your flies can be manipulated to behave "naturally." An adept fly fisher, however, can make the same magic happen with 4X, 5X, or 6X, fluoro or mono.

Photo by Geoff Mueller

To fluoro or not to fluoro? Fluorocarbon tippets and leaders function differently than those built from monofilament. They each have their pros and cons.

Just for experiment sake, can the same be said for 15-pound Maxima in the hands of our extremely "adept" fly fisher? Obviously 15-pound tippet material will not thread through most of the dries and nymphs in the fly shop bin. But if it did, how would trout react to it? According to Cutter, and in what may be the most graphic tippet experiment of all time—they wouldn't, at all. On California's notoriously stingy Fall River, Cutter glued foot-long pieces of 15-pound Maxima to a handful of test subjects, including Hexagenia mayflies and hoppers. The trout, amazingly, rose to the funky bugs without hesitation. "But they really wouldn't if they were attached to your fly line, because it would be almost impossible to present those same flies naturally, without drag," Cutter says.

Aha! The dreaded D-word. Tippets are mostly equal when it comes to how trout see them in the water, but they are not equal when it comes to how they affect our flies. Or, better yet, how they may or may not impart drag into the system. When we dunk heads underwater and open eyes to what seems like another planet, what we assume are the most luminous rivers in the country, are actually rife with floating, drifting, ascending, and descending animates and inanimates of all kinds. Amidst the trout food contained in a river or stillwater is a cacophony of nonfood items, everything from pinecones, grass, leaves, and squirrel shit to our lines, leaders, tippets, split-shots, and flies. Any of this matter not connected to rod, reel, and fly fisher bounces through the water in a natural drift. When our flies move down the pipe unnaturally—midges swimming upstream, alien streamers beaming down from the sky—this can trigger a trout to avoid them, spook, or come down with instantaneous lockjaw.

By using a thinner tippet to reduce drag, or a nonslip mono loop knot to give your flies more natural movement, you gain an edge. As for the other accouterments in your rig, such as split-shot and indicators, they too show up well from underwater and are undoubtedly seen by trout. They are also good vehicles for helping get flies to trout, at precise depths in the water column, and keeping those flies in the zone longer. It's hard to say what a trout thinks of a Thingamobobber compared to a Thill indicator or a piece of heavily ginked yarn. Snorkeling underwater they all appear like strike indicators to us and whether or not a focused trout associates floating "indicator" with "hook-prick" is next to impossible to know. Trout will, however, spook from the splash and line-slap of most dredging-oriented indictor deliveries. The key to avoid this, obviously, is to not throw your junk directly on top of the fish. Yarn, being light and airy, also has much stealthier qualities than similar-size indicators built from plastics or hard foams. With yarn, you can initiate a cast closer to the fish, and get away with it in most cases. Black yarn shows a great silhouette on the water, which is easy to follow through your drift. Its drawbacks arise when you're carrying two or more BB split-shots, which will sink it, or when Wyoming winds decide to hammer you with 40 mph gusts, making it hard to cast.

Split-shot is another fly-fishing accessory we use and one that trout are accustomed to seeing in the river. Depending on water clarity, split-shot shows up well in the underwater world. But like everything else rolling along the river bottom—cobblestone, sediment, and debris—it's hard to believe they look too out of place to discerning trout. In fact, split-shot is more likely to be sampled by curious trout rather than sparking a fight-or-flight response. When I spoke to Cutter at his home in California, he had recently been editing a section of underwater film footage. Over a twenty-minute span of tape, he counted fifteen fish "tasting" the split-shot—weight placed approximately 3 or 4 inches from his fly. Cutter paints his split-shot red in order to see it in play-back mode. Whether or not trout mistook the shot for an egg is not beyond the realm of possibility. But what they did not mistake it for was something that might lead to a catch-and-release outcome.

I've experienced similar instances using a swivel for weight above my tippet and chironomid patterns on BC Interior stillwaters. In many instances trout will taste and sample the swivel, marking the time to switch patterns to an appropriately colored fly—a Chromie tied with flat tin-sel, for instance. "Fish sample all this stuff," Cutter says. "And I believe split-shot doesn't make one wit of a dif-ference to them. And I tie my split-shot really close to the fly, because I want it on the bottom with my bugs floating above it, anywhere from 3 to 7 or 8 inches from the fly."

Back on the Bighorn, we were greeted with heavy wind and intermittent Baetis that popped en masse during the lulls. The headwind made casting a challenge. And with the axe-like swing of a 5-weight smashed into a frothing waterbed, any hopes of delicacy died. Soon my false-casts began to whistle. I'd heard that off-tune song before and I knew its meaning: tippet wad, one that would involve Johns Hopkins-like surgery to fix and re-fish. I also knew that my fingers were too cold to untangle it, and the fish were eating, and I could see snowdrifts barreling toward me from upriver. So instead of clipping and re-tying, I cast the mess into the melee of rising browns and watched as a fish committed suicide on an Adams buried deep inside a web of 4X tippet. I released the fish and met the guys downstream, who all no coincidence caught fish, too—on the 6X tippets I could do without.

This is not the case everywhere. The Frying Pan River sits in the heart of Colorado's Roaring Fork Valley. Its headwaters stem from the Sawatch Mountains in the White River National Forest, where the river once flowed unimpeded through most of its course. Ruedi Dam was constructed in the late '60s as part of the Fryingpan-Arkansas water diversion and delivery project, creating a massive mid-river impoundment in the form of Reudi Reservoir. In the ensuing years, one of the country's most coveted tailwaters formed below it. The dam outlet is located about 15 miles upstream of the town of Basalt. At the top sits the famed "Toilet Bowl" section—a deep bucket, housing double-digit fish that pork up on mysis shrimp. Where the Toilet Bowl flushes out, the river widens into a long, even-paced flat loaded with browns, rainbows, cutthroat, and brook trout. The river boasts thousands of fish per river mile in this brief tailwater reach—and on any given Sunday it seems like an equal amount of fly fishers, too.

People catch behemoth fish in the Fryingpan fairly regularly. And in addition to mysis shrimp, eggs, stoneflies, and mayflies of all stripes, the Pan is a technical midge fishery that requires #20 and smaller bugs to fish it effectively. Over the years, and in accordance with the constant barrage of fly chuckers through four seasons, imitations have gotten smaller (more exacting) and so too have tippet diameters. When fishing subsurface with minute imitations, this is a 6X fluorocarbon tippet river if you want a fighting chance at hooking these ultrakeyed-in fish.

During a visit in January 2011, our entourage arrived in the morning hours to ice-crusted banks and fifteen pickups vying for riverside parking at Reudi. The fishing and catching, for us at least, was hit and mostly miss. We found trout positioned everywhere in the river, including plenty within a 4-foot radius around our frozen toes. We fished an arsenal of #22-24 Rojo Midges, RS2s, Zebra Midges, eggs in Oregon cheese and chartreuse, mysis shrimp, you name it. Moreover, the day proved to be a perfect experiment in fishing most every fly known to man, but it wasn't until we messed with tippet size and tuned our presentations that we began to see results. Frying Pan trout have been privy to most every fly nuance and variation available over the course of their tailwater lifespan, and even on a dreary winter day they were feeding heavily—which was made apparent by flashing sides, savage top-water takes, and winking maws that we'd sometimes spot with the help of polarized shades.

Sticking to the knowledge of what we know trout can and can't see, I tied on several fly combinations with my trusty 4X and went fishless for several casts. Eventually I caved and paired down to 6X and 7X tippets. Takes came more consistently and, better yet, when we dropped strike indicators from our gangly nymph rigs and focused efforts on sight-fishing to specific feeders, the river came to life.

Veteran Taylor Creek fly shop guide Gifford Maytham has been fishing the Pan since 1992. When he first moved to the valley from Vermont he soon found his dream fish in the form of a 7-pound rainbow swimming circles in the Toilet Bowl. Today his goal is less about personal conquest and more about putting similarly absurd fish in the hands of clients. In order to do that, Maytham and the cadre of guides who regularly work the Pan have been forced to evaluate techniques and tweak rigs to get the job done in the face of mounting fishing pressure.

How has the river changed since that first Toilet Bowl trout? "Big time," Maytham says. "When I started fishing it we had the winter season mostly to ourselves. Now, in the last three to five years, you can drive up on the gnarliest day ever and there's still plenty of people up there. Wintertime has turned into this kind of 'tough-guy' thing, where you're seeing a lot of younger dudes who aren't deterred."

The explosion in angler numbers has also had a direct correlation on how trout react to tippet size, and a mainstay winter formula of 6X and 7X tippets for subsurface egg and midge rigs has become the go-to. "I've gone as small as 7X," Maytham says. "I don't usually use 8X, but there are plenty of people who do." In fact, Varivas Midge Super Tippet is now available down to 12X—the smallest I can find from a named manufacturer. A tippet this small might make sense for fishing microscopic flies in #30 range, which is possible on the Pan, but not necessarily needed. (Thankfully it comes with a "Non-Stress" coating, which we can assume lessens the anxiety of lashing on grizzly fluff to an intangible wisp of next to nothingness.)

Like Cutter, Maytham agrees that tippet size alone is never a home run. Instead diameter is dictated by basic physics and the old adage that you can't fit a square peg through a round hole. "For fishing midges in the size 20 to 24 category, 4X won't thread as easily as smaller diameter tippets," he says. "You won't squeeze 4X or even most 5X through that #24 hook eye. I don't think the fish on the Pan are necessarily tippet shy and for me it's mostly about preaching presentation to my clients— but more so, you've got to match your tippet to the size of your fly."

· ·

Trout see tippet, strike indicators, and split-shot far differently than we see them. For us they are extensions of our line, our last connection to the fly and fish. Tippets aid in turning a dry fly over and split-shot helps fly fishers attain depth when fishing wet. We want strong tippets so we don't lose fish. And we require them to be thin to hopefully gain an advantage during surface and sub-surface drifts. The key to understanding tackle selection from a trout's perspective revolves around presentation: a focus on better deliveries and fishing our bugs as close to a naturally behaving fly as possible.

7 The Feeding Machine

On the Water (and under It) Observations

Life is too short to wonder where you hid your waffle maker.

—Paula Deen

Although trout are not high on the evolutionary tree of fishes, with every new season they prove they are smart enough to outwit us. Understanding how and what trout see helps our cause. Another key to enlightenment is understanding a trout's focus when it comes to the dinner bell. Unlike humans, who dine specifically to romance, out of boredom, out of cultural ritual, to feed obnoxious emotions, and to meet vanity goals in the gym or on the scale, trout are wise enough to avoid these moronic pitfalls.

"Trout are not out there snacking," Brian Chan says. "They feed until they're full and then they slide off feeding areas back into deeper water or cover to relax." With that in mind, good fishing means good timing, and the right timing often coincides with the detonation of hatches producing steady streams of food to maintain their fitness, as well as population numbers. Because population numbers are related to available food sources, suitable habitat for the food source is essential. Macroinvertebrates such as mayflies, caddisflies, and stoneflies depend on nutrient-rich ecosystems as much as trout do. "Without the optimal substrate and habitat parameters in place, a stream cannot host a productive and abundant variety of aquatic insects, and without the essential ecological elements being present in the riverine corridor, we cannot accomplish the ultimate goal of building a productive fishery with large populations of healthy trout," says ERC's Troy Thompson.

Trout are opportunistic feeders that rely on various food items throughout the year. Trout inhabiting streams with a significant amount of riparian vegetation often feed heavily on terrestrials, such as grasshoppers, ants, and beetles. Riffles hold bottom-dwelling aquatic invertebrates, such as mayflies, caddis, and crustaceans. Additional food sources include invertebrates such as plankton, crustaceans, snails, sow bugs, scuds, and

Selectism. Trout may be opportunistic feeders but there is rhyme and reason behind their rhythms. Good fishing means good timing—which often coincides with meeting and matching a hatch.

leeches, as well as small fish, and eggs from spawning activity. Fat, happy trout are able to overwinter—when their forage base becomes scarce—thanks to the energy derived from these sources. This energy also gives them an edge when it's time to mate and reproduce.

Trout also require adequate cover to thrive and survive. Key ingredients include undercut banks, overhanging vegetation, turbulent or deep holding water, submerged debris, aquatic vegetation, root wads, oxygenated riffle sections, slower glide areas, gravel spawning beds, aquatic and riparian cover and, of course, available food sources, which are all key habitat components needed for sustainable, productive fisheries. The more habitat diversity, the more food sources, ambush zones to hammer smaller prey, and room for various species of trout to spread out and establish niches within the river. The riparian corridor is just as important to a productive fishery, providing essential staging foliage for the trout's food sources and completing a properly functioning ecosystem through the entire river corridor.

· ·

Depending on environmental circumstances, trout are capable of packing on about a pound a year. In productive environments a pound and a half—or up to 3 inches—is possible. Anything more than that, which isn't totally unheard of in rivers and lakes with exceptional forage bases, requires an extended growing season and year-round, hatch-friendly water temperatures, such as those found in tailwaters. Because trout suffer from a real lack of fast food outlets and catering options, that doesn't mean they're any less lazy than us when it comes to eating. But they're opportunists for a reason. Feeding behavior in the wild is a well-documented matter of expending the least amount of energy for the greatest caloric return. Trout feed like this in order to store energy for essential activities like sexual maturation, spawning, and to avoid predation. The less energy trout burn sourcing food, the more they have in the reserve tank for these other life-sustaining factors. This tidbit translates directly to fishing, because the more energy you put into timing and locating hatches—and feeding fish when they are most prone to dine—the more you increase your catching odds.

With building better odds on the brain, Tim Romano and I visited the University of Colorado in the winter of 2012, where we met PhD student/fly-fishing maniac, Tommy Detmer. Detmer's current hometown is Denver, but as a teenager he frequented Upstate New York's Adirondack State Park, where he volunteered at the Cornell Field Research Station. In addition to bird-dogging native brookie ponds and scouring tannin-stained Adirondack stillwaters for lunker lakers, Detmer immersed himself in fisheries science, learning how chemistry, different species of fish, and watershed characteristics might impact his fishing success. "My interest in fishing expanded to include curiosities in lake and stream ecosystems," he says. "I realized that I wanted to learn not only about fish, but about the systems in which fish live. I was already on my way to becoming a limnologist [the study of inland waters], though I didn't know it at the time."

When we met Detmer he was wrapping up his studies at CU's Department of Ecology and Evolutionary Biology. The brunt of his research had been focused on how fish introductions in high-elevation lakes altered food webs and the flow of nutrients. To gather data, Detmer and his colleagues hiked to lakes in Rocky Mountain National Park, where they collected and analyzed water, bugs, and fish samples. After several years of returning to the park and documenting his findings, Detmer's understanding of how trout see and react to food is about as honed as it gets. So we pried a little deeper.

Physiologically, Detmer says, trout are designed to be opportunistic feeders. For instance, if they see something that is edible and they haven't eaten in a while they will likely attempt to eat it. Therefore, you don't see physiological reactions to anticipated eating, like increased activity in salivary glands or gastric juices like you see in humans. Metabolism in fish is determined by a few factors. "Anticipation to feed is not one of those factors because fish are opportunistic," Detmer says. "For trout, and generally speaking, the primary factors that determine metabolism or activity are temperature, body size, and starvation level—when they last ate." It takes trout more energy to metabolize food when they are full, rather than on an empty stomach, which according to Detmer is important to fish selectivity in terms of choosing whether to chase a Muddler Minnow down or not.

At prime in-stream temperature ranges, trout will move for a meal. This sea-run cutt from Washington's Sol Duc River spied a big bite and committed.

The effect of temperature on metabolism is species specific. But for all trout, when water temps dip below a certain point it becomes more energetically *inefficient* to waste energy on movement, and the same thing happens above a certain temperature level. The survival range for trout is approximately 35° to 75°F, and the optimal feeding range for most species is documented at between 50 and 68 degrees, although cutthroat and brook trout have been noted to feed at slightly cooler temperatures. With those numbers in mind, it's no coincidence that optimal feeding temperatures for trout also coincide with prime hatch instigating temps. Early and late season mayflies such as Baetis begin hatching when water temps reach the mid to high 40s. As temperatures ramp up through spring and early summer, stoneflies and caddis join the mix. And when water temperatures consistently hit the low to mid 50s, hatch events for myriad species ensue and increased trout activity follows.

Prior to these hatches, we don't know whether or not trout have the capability to anticipate what's ahead. That is to say, trout are not dreaming about salmonflies a month leading up to their occurrence come June on central Oregon's Deschutes River. But when the nymphs begin their migration from river bottom to streamside vegetation, and when a full-fledged hatch takes flight over the ensuing days or weeks, trout, of course, key in and are quick to acclimate and react accordingly. Detmer says that although trout can't anticipate, they do become habituated to daily patterns. The famous Green Drake hatch on Penns Creek, near Coburn, Pennsylvania, for instance, presents a crisis for many anglers. When the apocalyptic spinner fall crashes the water at dusk, the river boils with rising fish, but there are so many competing naturals that hook-up rates are often low. Prior to dusk, there might be a handful of adults on the water and Para Drakes and Parachutes in the appropriate size and color will turn fish. I've often caught more fish during this non-hatch period, searching likely water for browns that are in the process of hatch "habituating."

Detmer explains: "If over the course of a couple of days there is a hatch at around 2 p.m., fish will typically pick up on that pattern and start to move into feeding lanes around that time. This could be interpreted as staging, but I would describe the movement as more habituated than anticipated." Moreover, when trout see increased activity in a macroinvertebrate group as it begins to move off the sediment to emerge they start keying in on this activity. "Again, this could be perceived as anticipation for a hatch," Detmer says, "but I think this could also be described more as reactionary than anticipatory. An example of trout being habituated feeders is when they have recently been stocked. They are so accustomed to feeding on pellets that you can throw small gravel bits in and see trout come to the area in 'anticipation' of feeding time."

Trout, like most fish, rely heavily on sight and are visual predators. The factors that determine the selectivity of trout are influenced in large part by species, fishing pressure, if the water is flowing or stagnant, and if the target is moving or stationary. Food preference is both complex and simple at the same time. General patterns in selectivity have been studied and documented. Basically, if you have a predator and two prey items available, and prey item A is preferred over prey item B, and if prey items A and B have equal availability and are similar in size, then trout will choose prey item A. However, if prey item B is more abundant than A, trout often show a stronger tendency to eat B, even though they actually prefer A. "This sounds contradictory at first," Detmer says, "but think about it this way: If you were starving and you were used to your food coming in a certain way— for instance, on a plate as opposed to being plopped on a super clean table, even though the food would be no different if it was on the table rather than on the plate,

Photo by Geoff Mueller

What's hatchin'? For trout, food preference is both complex and simple at the same time. At the most basic level, focus on what's readily available and you'll always be a step ahead of the game.

we would prefer the plate. This is because we have been conditioned to expect it on a plate."

In other words, if prey A—the preferred food—is glued to the surface of a stagnant eddy, while a plethora of prey B—the lesser preference—is streaming toward a trout along a conveyor belt of steady current, you want to match B. Similarly, during multiple-hatch scenarios, where two or more bugs are found on the water simultaneously, feed the trout what it wants first. But also consider where and how it wants it. What exactly do trout want when it comes to this feeding regime? Ultimately, it's a matter of what's going to put fuel in the tank and, when there's more than one option on (or in) the water, what snack will generate the best mileage after intake. Some macroinvertebrates offer better energy return than others, and this is a determining factor in prey selection. Organisms that are larger have more calories in them than lesser-size options. This predator-prey relationship can be modeled by calculating the ratio of energy return over energy expended for a particular food item. This theory is also important in terms of travel time to a prey item. "The trout calculates, not consciously of course, will its caloric return from an item exceed its caloric expenditure?" Detmer says. Another consideration is the length-to-mass relationship, which is a power function where larger (in terms of length) bugs are worth somewhere between a square and a cubic function more in terms of energy. Bigger bugs produce more energy, say a #6 salmonfly over a #22 midge, but when those midges are in abundance and easy pickings, their caloric return may trump chasing a solitary "big bug" half a mile down river. As for moving to feed, this again is dictated by whether or not trout are habituated, in this case for moving to feed. If a trout knows it can move to find food at a lower cost than sitting in an area and feeding, then it will choose to do that.

. . . .

In addition to hatch activity, there are other environmental factors that trigger feeding activity. Water temperature determines trout metabolism and activity level and is specific to each species of trout. The other major determinant hinges on light conditions. Piscivorous trout (or fish eaters) like bull and some brown trout tend to have a higher level of activity during low-light periods because prey are less likely to successfully evade a predator during these times. More insectivorous-inclined trout, like cutthroat and some rainbows, generally tend to have higher levels of activity during periods when insects are more active. It's also interesting to note that most freshwater insects evolved in the presence of fish for millions of years. And they too have adapted strategies to bolster safety from fishes, such as increased activity during low-light periods.

According to Detmer, many aquatic insect species—particularly Baetis and chironomids—increase their activity at night to avoid predation. "Think about it this way," he says. "If you were a caveman and you knew that saber-toothed tigers rely on sight to find you, would you go out more during the day or night?" Insects don't have the ability to think, instead they act according to behaviors that are imprinted in their DNA. But the same concept is true. Insects that are active when they are in the presence of predators—such as trout—are more likely to be eaten, unless they can overwhelm them in numbers, which is often the case with some of the heavier daytime hatches we see in the West.

Another consideration is age. Juvenile trout feed differently than older trout, and as anglers we must pay attention to these nuances—especially when it's the big one you're after. According to Detmer, the reason is twofold. First, wild fish have the capacity to learn. "Learned behavior in trout," he says, "is the result of millions of years of evolution in highly variable environments. Fish must learn to survive in unique environments: Each stream is not the same and each pool in each stream is not the same." Therefore, evolution has favored the individuals that have best adapted to these variables. The ability to learn makes trout effective in more diverse environments—to a limit. Second, metabolism acts differently—but in a very calculable way—in larger fish than smaller fish of the same species. Those varying metabolisms in large vs. small trout, play a large part in how they see and respond to food.

Detmer uses the analogy of a mouse and a moose to illustrate the phenomenon. Small bodies like those of mice, he says, burn ten times as much chemical energy to heat per unit time as do larger massed organisms, like a moose. The result is that large mammals can survive much longer on their chemical stores than small ones. In the case of a mouse and a moose, this difference is greater than tenfold based on the following calculations:

Time required to release an amount of energy equal to its internal reserves:

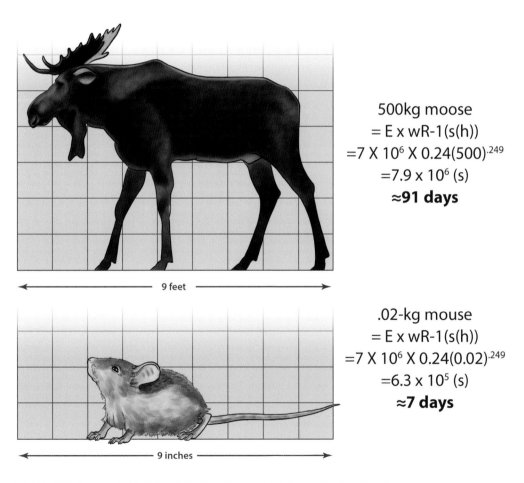

500kg moose
$$= E \times wR\text{-}1(s(h))$$
$$= 7 \times 10^6 \times 0.24(500)^{.249}$$
$$= 7.9 \times 10^6 \, (s)$$
≈91 days

← 9 feet →

.02-kg mouse
$$= E \times wR\text{-}1(s(h))$$
$$= 7 \times 10^6 \times 0.24(0.02)^{.249}$$
$$= 6.3 \times 10^5 \, (s)$$
≈7 days

← 9 inches →

These calculations help explain why bigger fish are considered "wary." And, yes, fish are not mammals but the coefficients are similar, so you see the same general trends.

To put this mouse vs. moose scenario into trout terms, think of it this way: A small trout must consume more energy, much more, to grow and survive than a larger trout of the same species. Thus your typical trophy trout—anything more than 18 inches long, for example—can rely on its chemical stores longer and in turn feed less frequently. Moreover, the myth of the "old wary trout" may just be that, a myth. Although fish are instinctually wary when it comes to predators, such as you and I, they are not necessarily "wary" when it comes to eating—if and when environmental conditions are right. Large trout have the luxury of feeding less, which mathematically makes them harder to catch. To add insult to injury, they are typically found in less abundance in any given trout stream or stillwater. Both factors attribute to the fact that fly fishers on average—Joe Humphreys and Landon Meyers of the world not included—catch more small trout than large. Small trout are simply wired to feed at will. And if that large, old humpback brown is more prone to a piscivorous diet, and more inclined to indulge after dark, you too increase your chances by waiting until after campfire embers smolder, donning a headlamp, and wading into the wee hours. The odds are you'll find that fish, and he'll be happy . . . and hungry.

If night timing isn't your MO, do not fret. Large fish can and are found all day, every day when the right conditions combine with patience, persistence, and more importantly, an understanding of trout social hierarchies. By definition, hierarchies represent arrangement of items or objects—in this case trout—that are either above, below, or at the same level as one another. Trout do not form ranks as far as social status or business ambitions are concerned, but when it comes to dining, hierarchies develop around optimal positioning in a pool or feeding lane. And, you guessed it, the larger or largest trout in a pack of varying size fish often take prime positioning. "Generally," Detmer says, "the largest fish is in the alpha position, however, if you have different species the interaction can change. For example, in interactions between brook trout and cutthroat, a smaller brookie will sometimes outcompete a larger cutt. This only lasts up to a certain point and then the larger fish, no matter what the species, will assume the alpha position despite the different species present."

Hierarchy models show trout lining up linearly below the alpha in the pool, according to size. This is because alpha trout seek locations with optimal foraging conditions. Generally speaking, if your aim is to target the largest trout in a pack of rainbows slurping trico spinners on a September morning on the North Platte, the dimples may be similar in size, but the larger fish in the group

Two pool-feeding rainbows lined up in succession on Utah's Green River. Alpha trout, or the larger, healthier specimens in the pack, shoulder their way into optimal foraging position at the head, while lesser trout typically fall in behind.

Barometric Pressure and Phases of the Moon

It was a moon that could stir wild passions in a moo cow. A moon that could bring out the devil in a bunny rabbit. A moon that could turn lug nuts into moonstones, turn Little Red Riding Hood into the big bad wolf.
—Tom Robbins on full moons in *Still Life with Woodpecker*

What prompts trout to feed? In addition to the hatch scenarios presented here, there are other environmental factors worth paying attention to. When fishing turns sour, barometric pressure is a commonly cited influence. Take, for example, five days booked camping, floating, and fishing Montana's Smith River. It's the third week of July and you're greeted with a favorable, steady weather pattern of blue skies and surface air temperatures in the mid to upper 70s. You spend days one and two throwing gangly hoppers and Chubby Chernobyls to happy browns that hammer them with confidence.

But on day three something runs afoul. The weather is similar to days one and two: clear skies, pleasantly warm. You throw the same flies to similar lies but the trout are dour and off the bite. You look over to your friend casting from the bow of your 14-foot inflatable raft and ask, "What's up?" He turns back to you and responds, "Must be the barometer." The barometer? Yes, of course it *must* be the barometer, you

both nod in agreement, hiding the fact that in actuality you have no idea what that means. But it sure sounds good. And the river sure isn't fishing right. So you go with it.

In reality, the influences of barometric pressure, or a rising or falling barometer, on trout feeding behavior is not some myth or an excuse made up by guides to cover their butts on days when clients can't catch fish. Here's why: Barometric pressure has a significant impact in relation to a trout's air bladder organ. A trout's air bladder, or swim bladder, is connected to its esophagus and helps control buoyancy, so a trout can suspend, ascend, or burp and descend, without wasting energy. The swim bladder helps anchor trout in an upright position in the water column and it's also highly sensitive to changes in barometric pressure.

When the barometer crashes, it essentially means ugly weather is en route. Trout can feel these changes in the air/water interface. When they do, they can go off the bite. This phenomenon can equal terrible fishing and someone scratching their head, then shrugging their shoulders, then claiming, "Barometer's dropping!" followed by everyone in the boat nodding in agreement.

Another real, oft-cited, and mostly misunderstood influence on fish feeding is moon phase. Trout during a full moon have been noted to feed through the night—if and when there is hatch activity or forage base that will sustain that kind of activity. Some Western caddis hatches, *Brachycentrus* or grannom caddis for instance, are famous for prolific hatches that prompt late-night feeding. And on full moon cycles trout will continue to eat until the sun rises the following morning. This full-moon feeding phenomenon can lead to poor daytime fishing, considering trout that have gorged during dark will

be less prone to feed heavily during the day. The first several days of full moon influence has the greatest effect on fish behavior. Leading up to a full moon. The first week after the fact, is a window often associated with good fishing.

Ultimately, like most debated trout fishing phenomena, there is no hard and fast rule that says fishing around a full moon will be horrendous. In fact, targeting a full moon during the summer and early fall months is a great time to pick up large browns on mouse patterns at night. We've experimented with mouse patterns extensively over the past several seasons throughout Colorado and Wyoming. The scenario goes something like this: After a day of fishing we retreat to the campfire where many beers are consumed and killed, a whiskery rodent with a hook protruding from its rear is plucked from

Photo by Kat Yarbrough

Targeting a full autumn moon opens up opportunities to mouse around for large browns after dark.

a fly box, and someone comes up with the brilliant idea to stumble down to the river and chuck it.

The best mouse fishing I have seen came by way of a cloud-washed September harvest moon on Colorado's Yampa River. Our group included Ross Purnell and Steve Hoffman of *Fly Fisherman* magazine and Colorado locals Landon Mayer and John Barr. With headlamps blaring we trekked from the house to a long riffle that dumped into a deep run abutting a steep, bouldered bank. During the day we had fished midge dries to selective sippers. But for this mission we tied on foam and deer-hair skaters—the Morrish Mouse—and rolled several nocturnal browns, including a 25-inch behemoth, one of the burliest I've seen landed on the Yampa to date.

As for day-time conditions, don't let any discussion of "bad moon rising" omens sway you too far from fishing during full-moon cycles. There are anomalies to every fishing scenario, and great fishing can certainly be found. On a recent December morning, I stuffed the rear of the 4Runner with rods, reels, boxes of streamers and wets, extra layers, and Hatch—fishing buddy Tanner Irwin's bone-sniffing Labrador retriever—en route to the Miracle Mile stretch of the North Platte River.

At about noon the streamer bite soured, which is normally the case on this off-color tailwater, as midges pop and trout key in on the emergence. At 4 p.m. the wind spiked, the sun dropped from the sky, and temperatures hit subzero. At that moment a buttery brown hen with a solar system of halos painted across her icy-blue cheeks latched onto my streamer at midswing. As the sky darkened a perfect full moon crested an empty Wyoming landscape— one clearly capable of turning lug nuts into moonstones.

will form the ones upstream of the lesser-size fish. Bingo. Detmer says this behavior is exclusive of the territoriality concept, which involves exclusivity of an area. Bluegill are a prime example of this because they will defend defined spaces for both food and spawning territory. "Trout on the other hand will allow the passage of other fish in their area but prefer to be in a hierarchy," Detmer says. "This rule does not apply to waters that have been stocked because as much fun as stocked fish are to catch, they are stupid and don't act according to natural rules."

8 John McMillan: Enter Anadromy

To comprehend the evolutionary history of trout and salmon, one must take a perspective completely removed from ordinary human experience. One must think not only in millions of years, but in tens and even hundreds of millions of years.

—Robert J. Behnke, *Trout and Salmon of North America*

Tim Romano and I found the Olympic Peninsula on a Thursday night in late September. We'd hopped the West Seattle Ferry from Fauntleroy to Southworth, picked up two new snorkels in Bremerton, hiked 8 miles to catch one half-dead pink salmon on the Dungeness River, dined on mediocre Mexican in Port Angeles, all en route to the eerie hamlet of Forks, Washington.

In addition to its stellar steelheading rep, Forks has recently become synonymous with a certain *Twilight* series, as it plays an integral home-base role in the onscreen teen-lust drama. This becomes apparent when you roll into town, greeted by signs for "Liquor," "Smoked Salmon," and "Twilight Tours"—all bedecking the same building. As we moved deeper into the mossy landscape, a half moon rose over Crescent Lake, a thick mist poured in from the west, and a savage Coastal Range enveloped us.

From the front seat of a rattling Rent-A-Wreck, the wilds of the OP seemed like a logical place to run into something supernatural. Vampires, or possibly Bigfoot. We crossed the Elwha River (at that time undergoing remedial work in the form of major dam removal projects), the Sol Duc, then the Calawah, and my thoughts swerved to coastal cutts and steelhead and our upcoming meeting with area fisheries biologist John McMillan. As we pulled into the Olympic Suites parking lot, I wondered whether McMillan might be one of those *Twilight* nuts, too. But I had a sneaky suspicion, John—being the son of legendary steelheader and vocal, local conservationist, Bill McMillan—preferred chasing fish over the local fangfare.

. . . .

John McMillan spends an inordinate amount of time with trout. And his relationship with coastal cutthroat and wild steelhead populations of Washington's Olympic Peninsula region runs deep. For instance, there's a 20-pound steelhead hen on a stretch of the Sol Duc River that McMillan knows intimately. Well, not like that, but he was there when, for days on end, she turned sideways, refurbishing the river floor with an undulating tale and cobbling together a deep redd to rear her offspring. That first redd was rejected for inadequacies we'll never know, and the hen went to work contouring a second, third, and fourth—finally settling on one worthy of her brood. While we're walking the riverbank, McMillan points out her industrious efforts. The hen has long since left the scene. Her progeny, however, will cling to it like home, fatten up from smolts to juveniles, then eventually follow Mom's path back to the ocean with spring freshet. McMillan will be there to see their return.

After a rendezvous at a local Forks gasmart, we meet McMillan and head toward the Calawah River. It's July, and early as far as anadromous runs of salmon and steelhead are concerned. Coastal and resident cutthroat rule the kingdom. As the morning fog lifts, McMillan ties on a large October Caddis dry with a spun deer-hair head and wades upstream to a set of choppy riffles that pour into a dark, deep run. The cutthroat are stupid for the October

Fisheries biologist John McMillan stands in the now-vacated redd of a 20-pound steelhead hen on a wet day in coastal Washington. McMillan has clocked many hours snorkeling rivers across the Olympic Peninsula and beyond. If the fish are in, bet that he knows where.

Caddis. And as McMillan shotguns the river with casts they return fire, taking aim at his fly. After a couple of hours of this, we uproot and hit another river section, this one with a steep fir-lined path that offers limited traction. At the bottom of the slip-and-slide, we find a river split in two by a downed tree. Tim and I follow McMillan up and over, through a heavy push of water, and onto a mid-river gravel bar. There we have two choices: up or downstream. Although we came for cutts, McMillan tells us this is our best chance for a steelhead. He should know; he swims this section of river regularly as a contract fisheries biologist for NOAA. I choose the path of least resistance: downstream. McMillan, wasting no time, bids us farewell and good luck. With his head down he purposefully sidesteps the belly of the long slow pool colored by last night's rain. He jets to the head of the run. Twitches that deer-hair bug. And proceeds to hook something more dramatic than the 10- to 14-inch cutts that had been the flavor of the morning. It's a chrome steelhead hen, about 5 or 6 pounds, and when I arrive upstream I find it on the bank. "These hatchery fish shouldn't be here," McMillan says matter-of-factly. "But my wife will appreciate it." We shrug our shoulders and keep fishing.

In about two more months, the brunt of the hatchery steelhead runs will enter this system and other OP mainstays such as the Hoh and Bogachiel rivers. They will be joined by the march of wild winter-run steelhead, starting in January and continuing through February, March, and even April. Together they will join sea-runs and resident cutthroat, as well as population pockets of resident rainbows. Together in the stew, they will all compete for space, habitat, forage, and prime staging and spawning positioning come spring. The life cycle will be completed for some and begin for others.

This much is known. But for fisheries scientists like McMillan, a fascinating unknown variable entered the mix in 2012. It came in the form of dam removal on the Elwha

River, a system with strong resident rainbow trout populations that began thriving after the construction of the
Elwha and Glines Canyon dams between 1913 and 1927.
The dams effectively cut off chinook, pink, chum, sock-
eye, and coho salmon, as well as steelhead and sea-run
cutts from nearly 70 miles of traditional spawning habitat in the cold, fast-running reaches of the upper river
and its tributaries. Subsequently, fish stocks have been
reduced to a shadow of their pre-dam heyday. Estimates
place pre-dam adult salmon returns at nearly 400,000
fish. With the dams in place, less than 1 percent of those
fish returned to the river.

McMillan, who lives on the Elwha River, had fly fished
and studied it for years leading to the 5-year fishing moratorium imposed in 2012. The fishing pause was enacted
to allow Elwha salmonid populations to take hold and
recover after dam deconstruction. Prior to that, most of
McMillan's fishing on the Elwha involved driving about 5
miles upstream and targeting the water between dams,
where resident rainbows averaged small size because
of their prolific numbers confined within a tight space.
Snorkeling this same stretch, the biggest fish McMillan has witnessed pushed 20 inches and the biggest he
has caught measure about 16 inches, typically fishing a
3-weight and throwing an Elkhair Caddis.

In addition to fishing and snorkeling, McMillan works
with NOAA to help analyze river data. Being the sole
NOAA representative in the Port Angeles area, he essentially works alone. The job entails close consultation
with the Lower Elwha Tribe, daily fieldwork measuring
river turbidity, conducting redd counts for steelhead and
rainbow trout, and basic health and habitat monitoring.
Once a month a group of Seattle biologists travel to the
Elwha to conduct intensive studies, donning snorkels
and masks and sampling fish to learn how fast they grow,
what their condition factor and diets are comprised of,
and how their river density, composition, and distribution

will be affected by dam removal. Prior to deconstruction, it had been native species such as rainbow, bull, and some introduced brook trout inhabiting water above the dams. That is now poised to change.

Dam removal presents a unique set of circumstances for resident trout. During the fall of 2011, the Elwha River removals received a substantial number of pages in the press. Articles appeared in *National Geographic,* the *Seattle Times*, *Washington Post, New York Times* and, closer to home, in *The Drake* and *Fly Fish Journal*. The deconstruction efforts had also been woven into subject matter for several documentaries, including one by Felt Soul Media—makers of the award-winning environmental epic *Red Gold*, highlighting the Pebble Mine

Dam deconstruction presents unique opportunities for resident trout populations to reconvene with their former anadromous cousins. The author makes a cast for sea-run cutts in an undammed swirl of Washington's Olympic National Park.

fight in Alaska's Bristol Bay region. Patagonia Company founder Yvon Chouinard, and other vocal anti-dam proponents, spoke about the precedent-setting implications on the Elwha, and the domino effect that might reverberate throughout the Columbia and Snake River drainages. Other environmental stakeholders spoke against hatchery-supplemented steelhead runs on the Elwha, including author Dylan Tomine, who wrote that, "Sad as it may be, it's time to stop putting cookies out on Christmas Eve and tucking teeth under pillows. We have to grow up and face the facts: Hatcheries don't work."

What much of this heartfelt cry for wild steelhead and salmon recovery didn't mention, however, is the result it would have on native trout already thriving within the Elwha system. These species and their survival before and after dams and, moreover, with the re-introduction of anadromous species, marked McMillan's energetic focus.

"We're trying to see how anadromy will influence these fish, and what we've done is developed a series of hypotheses to quantify the results from the subsequent changes in habitat, such as alteration to food base and distribution," McMillan says.

"The dam removal released a ton of trapped sediment, so we expect the macroinvertebrate populations to change, too. The Elwha will likely shift significantly, losing much of its predominantly cold, clean-water attributes and its prolific stonefly and mayfly populations in the short term. We're going to lose a lot of this in certain areas as the sediment works its way through the system."

In the long term, nature will be forced to work itself out. Future fishing opportunities remain an unknown entity. But that doesn't stop one from speculating. Biologists suspect that steelhead will outcompete resident trout because they will produce a much higher density of offspring, earlier. If this is the case, resident trout populations will decline, substantially, because there is only so much food and space available in the Elwha system. In addition to steelhead, chinook, pink, and chum salmon also enter the shoulder-room equation—but McMillan says these species will have less influence on trout. Coho, however, which utilize similar shallow-water rearing channels, and eat rainbow fry, will be influential.

But it's not all doom and gloom for resident trout populations. In fact, the weeding out of smaller fish in the race for survival should leave a more robust remaining population. Competition will weed out small fish and lead to bigger, healthier, stronger rainbows. McMillan adds, "We'll see what we see in a lot of anadromous systems, where rainbows start maturing at 12 to 13 inches rather than 8. And I presume we'll have some rainbow up to and over 20 inches because we'll have a lot more protein coming down the pipe in the form of salmon eggs and their nutrient-rich decomposition."

Today, much of this trout survival analysis boils down to the spawn, and how resident rainbow trout reproduction will be affected by an influx of steelhead pouring in and on top of them. Egg size is essential to survival. The bigger the egg, the more fat it contains, and the higher the likelihood it will survive its first month out of the gravel. Although steelhead and resident rainbows have similar size eggs, rainbows are at a marked disadvantage when it comes to output.

On the lower Elwha, before the dams were removed, biologists electro-shocked a small swath of river where steelhead resided. They found several hundred young-of-the-year trout (fish that had just spawned and hatched that year) about the length of your pinky finger. But in the upper water where no steelhead resided, a similar-size river sample yielded about half that many rainbows, typically about 35 mm to 45 mm in length. The reason for the anomaly is a matter of simple mathematics. Steelhead have the ability to produce more eggs: 3,000 to 5,000 compared to a few hundred contained within an average-size female rainbow. Steelhead also spawn about three months earlier and dig deeper redds, diminishing the chance for mortality during the river-bottom scouring effects of run-off.

By spawning early, steelhead have a leg up in the growth department and with dams removed, resident rainbows will be at a disadvantage. But it's one that most steelheaders can live with. McMillan expects steelhead to be the dominant species in the Elwha system in years to come, even above chinook salmon, which once pushed the 100-pound mark. Why? Because "the Elwha is a steelhead watershed, man," McMillan says. "It's going to have summer runs, winter runs, and they're going to be big fish. When you look at the Elwha, it acts like a northern BC river. It is *mykiss* heaven, with big boulders and lots of great habitat."

· ·

Born "dirt poor" in "the middle of nowhere," John McMillan's backyard abutted Washington's Washougal River—a tributary of the Columbia. Family vacations consistently landed him on Oregon's Deschutes River, with a fly rod in hand. And his father, Bill, was and is a celebrated fisheries advocate connected by a blood bond to the steelhead arteries coursing through coastal Washington. These factors combined helped plant a seed, one that has branched into a career path and spurred a lifetime quest for answers to the proverbial fish riddle. Before females entered an ambitious prepubescent mind, McMillan's first love was *Oncorhynchus mykiss.* (In addition to a severe hankering for cutthroat trout.) What set his heart a flitter? More than anything, McMillan says, he was intrigued by a trout's innate ability to survive amid a constant barrage of adversities that span four seasons on a river.

Those curiosities manifested as McMillan became increasingly adept with a fly rod. He took a keen interest in trout distributions as they pertained to different Pacific

Northwest river systems. He wanted to know how, like on the Elwha, would those densities be affected by curveballs such as one of the largest dam removal projects in this country's history, and the movement of anadromous species into the resident trout mix. Over the past thirty years, he has spent more and more time underwater, moving from weekend childhood curiosities to obsessive eight-hour long winter snorkel surveys in subzero rivers as an adult.

The result? McMillan, more than most, possesses a keen understanding of how trout—and steelhead—react when presented with opportunity in the river environment. His trout behavior observations are remarkable. And when put in context, can help us all become better fishers. Or at least think more like the quarry we're set on seducing.

. . . .

McMillan's obsession started with a couple of feet of 12-pound Maxima. His nine-year-old hands gripped the large white spool, shifted the elastic band to loosen the tag end, stripped a section off, and snipped it. He then looped one end of the tippet to his finger and cinched a fly to the other. This basic set-up became the apparatus for McMillan's first underwater experiments. With it, he donned a mask and snorkel and dove head first into the river in search of willing research participants. The first focus group consisted of small cutthroat—10 to 12 inches long—that were undeterred by a kid kicking in the current and came right within view to sniff, peck, and, more often than not, eat the fly. Those first impressions centered on surprise: He couldn't believe how bold these trout were so close to human presence. His second impression was dismay: "You wouldn't believe how many takes we are missing," he says.

In addition to missed opportunities, a young McMillan was also able to determine fairly accurately what trout

Photo by Geoff Mueller

Releasing a winter run buck back into western Washington waters.

do and don't like based on their reactions to his subsurface fly presentations.

"The fish I witnessed were constantly on the grab, sampling food like fat kids at a buffet," he says. "They're trying all sorts of stuff," but one thing that stood out was their preference for pace. Insects moving at the same speed of the river, in a natural drift, got gobbled more than the rest. When his fly dragged or moved unnaturally it was shunned. But when he twitched the fly or made it act wounded, that imparted another reaction—one that got bit.

That first night, a nine-year-old McMillan went to sleep with his mind aswirl. After a restless few hours under the sheets, he rose early the next morning raring for an underwater follow-up. Wearing his mask and snorkel, he waded into the same hole as the day prior, with the same rig, in search of the same 10- to 12-inch cutts. The water was invigorating, and after getting acclimated he opened his goggle-housed eyes to a strange sight. There, swimming in the bowels of the run was a fish the size of a log. Instead of pursuing it like an otter and scaring it halfway back to the Pacific, McMillan hunkered down and gave it space. And within a few minutes the skittish steelhead relaxed. "And so I swung that Soft-Hackle in front of it and low and behold that son of a bitch took it right off my finger, with 2 feet of line out. It just snapped it right off," McMillan says. "I jumped out of the water and went running to my Dad, screaming 'Oh my god, a steelhead took it!'"

For McMillan, it was a watershed moment. He was young and not yet steelheading on his own, "but it definitely changed the way I approach trout."

That steelhead and those first cutthroat opened the door to an ongoing series of in-river experiments. By the time McMillan turned sixteen, he was still snorkeling the Washougal—expanding his understanding of underwater trout behavior—but he'd elevated the science and applied it to fishing applications. Steelhead, he learned, were smart. Like resident trout, they made mistakes, but they were quicker to learn from them. Many times after tasting the bite of a hook, steelhead backed up from it after subsequent swings through the run, smacking their maws open and shut like a dog with a mouthful of citrus. Because steelhead do their bulking up in the ocean, and are not necessarily searching for protein to survive in the river environment, their choices were more calculated and cunning. McMillan observed that resident trout on the other hand, constantly seeking food, were easier to entice. Again and again.

Today, after thousands of hours snorkeling, McMillan has a better perception of what is happening below the water. And it's upped his fishing game immensely. "I'm not as interested in what's happening on top. Instead I'm thinking, 'Is there a place where the fish can sit, not expend much energy, and how many buddies does he have around him?'" he says. "Sometimes you catch the small fish first. Sometimes you catch the big one. But ultimately there can be a number of fish vying for your fly at once, and they're not necessarily the one you want."

Back on the Calawah River with Tim and me, McMillan fishes fast, covering as much water as possible in search of The One. "If a fish bites, great. If not, move on. But there are certain situations and telltale indicators that— from being underwater—remind me to stop, slow down, and pay attention," he says. After all when those 10-inch cutthroat suddenly morph into a 10-pound steelhead, the fly attached to your rod has just as good a chance as the one dangling from the end of a nine-year-old's finger.

9 Building a Confidence Fly Box

Retired basketball coach and talented chair thrower Bobby Knight is adamant the best fish catcher ever mass-produced is Orvis's TeQueely Streamer. He made the claim in the spring of 2012 while speaking to an audience of guides, reps, and various industry types attending Simms' annual Ice Out event. Attendees had packed Bozeman's Wilson Auditorium to hear what the legendary coach had to say about fly fishing, basketball, and life. And in this moment of TeQueely head scratching, the snickering crowd hung on Knight's every syllable, anticipating a punch line that was never delivered. The TeQueely? Yes, said Knight, "It's the only fly you'll ever need."

Considering Knight led the US basketball team to Olympic gold in 1984 and has more than 900 NCAA Division I wins in his pocket, one can assume he knows something about winning formulas. And the TeQueely, in fact, may just be the sexiest bug ever to brush yellow rubber legs against the crinkled kype of an ornery old brown trout—if it's the only fly you were to ever fish. That's because the TeQueely (Parachute Adams, Pheasant Tail, Woolly Bugger, Muddler Minnow, Royal Wulff, RS2, and so on) is just one of many representatives that fall into the "confidence flies" category—those patterns that see reoccurring usage because they have and continue to work in the field. The reliability of confidence flies has been chiseled into the mind's eye, driving their powers of trout persuasion to the realm of sacred, irrefutable fact.

Here's another fact: my current fly portfolio does not include a single fucking TeQueely. But the collection has been whittled to a handful of confidence-inspiring flies: prime clumps of fur, feather, and synthetic materials that during specific situations consistently put happy times into my fish-slimed hands. As fly tiers continue to tweak, hammer, primp, fluff, streamline, swim, weigh, measure, dream, delight, and devise, the selection is in constant flux. But the following standbys have come to form the TeQueelys of my in-river experiences. And there's no doubt—in my mind—that they are the *best* six flies ever produced by some of the top contemporary fly tiers out there. I'll crack a chair to the curb in defiance of anyone who says otherwise, including Bobby Knight. Here are those bugs and why.

1. CHUBBY CHERNOBYL BY CHRIS CONATY, IDYLWILDE FLIES

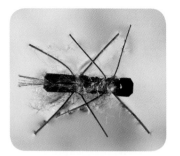

Chubby Chernobyl.

Hook: Dai Riki 730, #8-12
Thread: UTC Ultra 140 denier
Dubbing: SLF Kaufmann Golden Stone or Dave Whitlock Golden Brown
Tail: Crystal Flash
Foam: 2 mm tan craft foam
Wing: Synthetic poly
Legs: Sili Legs

Chris Conaty of Idylwilde Flies in Portland, Oregon, is hesitant to take credit for the sometimes-lambasted Chubby Chernobyl. The fly is basically a variation on the original Chernobyl Ant. Several years ago, Conaty received a custom order from a shop on the South Fork of the Snake River. It was for a black foam Chernobyl with a red dubbed body and black rubber legs. This pattern had no tail, the foam was attached to the hook shank in several places, and Conaty remembers it having one wing of either poly or Antron. He also remembers it being one of the ugliest damn flies he'd ever seen.

At the time, the team at Idylwilde was producing several Chernobyl variations, they were selling well, and there was chatter around the office about expanding the lineup. Conaty took a selection of materials, locked himself in the office, and started the process of Frankensteining a new bug. He dressed it up by adding flash to the tail. He tied in two wings to enhance its visibility. He added tail flash that made the fly modifiable to suit on-river demands. Similarly, the elongated double wings could be cut to alter its profile and ride. Square silicon legs were chosen instead of the round rubber ones because Conaty felt they caught more current, perhaps wiggled better, and he liked the sparse flecks of sparkle they contained. As for the name, that was simple. Upon twisting up the first batch, Conaty remarked that it looked just like a fat Chernobyl. Soon thereafter the Chubby Chernobyl was born.

The Chubby's original body color was gold, good for imitating local hopper hatches. But it proved to be much more than that when it was introduced to Deschutes River trout in the form of a floating gob of golden stonefly. Its success on the Deschutes launched it out of the ballpark. Idylwilde now moves thousands upon thousands of Chubby Chernobyls in various colors annually. It's a top seller across the board.

Fish love it. Fly fishers have either fallen under the same spell, or continue to love to hate it. But there is little question as to its effectiveness . . . other than the *why*. The debate as to what trout see when a #10 Chubby Chernobyl comes twirling overhead varies from camp to camp. Conaty has discussed the fly's merit with guides and outfitters at length and they, like him, have witnessed trout move long distances to choke down a Chubby, even when naturals are swimming closer by.

Oregon-based guide Brian Silvey says the Chubby's charm stems from the way its legs are tied in—crossed in the front and back, giving it movement similar to a natural trying to break the grip of the water's surface. Others say it works because it sits incredibly low, especially after the dubbing soaks in water and added weight. This is not unlike a lot of other dubbed flies, but the Chubby possesses the added bonus of a wing you can see, even when it's half submerged. Still others say it's the actual wing material and colors that dupe trout into seeing a tricked-out bug, itching to take flight.

"I've had multiple people highlight these three things, and rarely have they suggested it could be all of the above," Conaty says. "It's been fun to debate but I really have no idea what the answer is. In the end, it's so hard to tell."

Whatever the reason, or combinations of, Conaty has latched onto a winning formula with the Chubby Chernobyl. Look for olive Green Drake variations and a classic Royal Wulff color scheme of this ambidextrous fly in seasons to come.

2. HEMORRHOIDAL MOUSE BY FRANK SMETHURST, MONTANA FLY COMPANY

Hook: Gamakatsu B10S Stinger Hook
Thread: 3/0 tan
Tail: Med size chenille light brown
Hemorrhoid: Orange chenille
Body: Deer Hair

Hemorrhoidal Mouse.

In 2009 the film *Eastern Rises* introduced the greater fly fishing world to the mouse crushing antics of Russia's Kamchatka Peninsula rainbows. It has since become a cult classic and, much like earlier Felt Soul Media projects, such as *Running Down the Man*, it featured a central character by the name of Frank Smethurst. I mention the film because it also introduced us to Smethurst's furry little friend—a mouse pattern with a backseat flare-up of hemorrhoidal proportions.

The Hemorrhoidal Mouse is the product of roots that stem several years back before its cameo appearance on the big screen. Its development began in 1992 while Smethurst was guiding at Alaska's Katmai Lodge, with a mission to catch rainbows on mice later and later into the summer season. Typically Alaska rainbows hit the mouse throughout June, but as the salmon begin to spawn in July they become more transfixed on the underwater caviar streaming into the river.

Being an astute and observant angler, Smethurst retired mouse to box, set forth with an indicator and pegged egg, and fished. But something strange was brewing: In these attempts to deliver the egg subsurface, fish continually rose and annihilated his bobbing, bright-orange strike indicator. Being an aficionado of the mouse and a seasoned student of the egg, Smethurst quickly put two and two together and built the ultimate omelet. If giant Alaska rainbows wanted a floating egg, why not deliver it on the rear end of an ultrabuoyant, protein-laced mouse?

"It's the furthest thing from rocket science," Smethurst says. "I just basically took the principles of an egg-sucking leech and applied them to the surface, trailing a mouse."

To its creator, the new fly looked like a mouse carrying a briefcase full of eggs, but Mouse-Carrying-A-Briefcase-Full-Of-Eggs was a tough name to swallow. At Katmai, with the help of veteran guides such as Ed Ward, Scott Howell, Dec Hogan, and Scotty O'Donnell, the nameless fly soon received a new handle. "Someone decided the mouse had a problem, and that problem was similar to hemorrhoids," Smethurst says. "The name burned and it stuck."

The combination of mouse and bright-orange-hot-spot quickly proved its mettle that first season on the Katmai. It caught surface-oriented rainbows through July and August, even a few in September. But its greatest feat was yet to come. Several years later, after Smethurst had returned to the Lower 48, a second Hemorrhoidal outbreak occurred at the 2004 Fly Fishing Masters competition. During qualifiers in Steamboat Springs, Colorado, competitors were pitted against some monster fish of dubious origins, and tasked to tie a worthy fly right there, on the spot.

"The fish looked really big and stupid and kind of ravenous so I thought, 'Why not the mouse?'" Smethurst says.

The Hemorrhoidal became the winning ticket to the Montana-based finals by allowing Smethurst to "audition" and "cut" smaller trout and leaving it on the dinner plate for a big boy to scratch its mousy inclinations.

As a general order of flies, the greater fly-fishing community has and continues to largely ignore mouse patterns. They've been relegated to full moons in fall. And some of the more cartoonish variations—whiskers and beady little eyes—seem almost too cute to fish. Smethurst says it's a glaring oversight: "If you're really thinking about what terrestrials are important in a meadow, and you're looking at beetles and ants above mice, you're not seeing the forest for the trees. Certainly in the arid sections of Colorado, Montana, and Wyoming, I think the mouse is an absolutely golden approach during a remarkably consistent amount of time."

The Hemorrhoidal might not be the most exacting mouse pattern on the market, but it does several things right—number one being it throws a huge wake on the surface of the river that keep trout looking up. It achieves this with a splayed deer-hair overcoat with a trimmed underbody that rocks back and forth like a rickety old boat. The fly has a skating lip similar to gurgler-style patterns and its irresistible bright-orange butt is formed from Antron, egg yarn, or similar.

What do trout see staring into the hemorrhoidal rear end of a waking mouse? Most likely, something to cure the hunger.

"I think if any gamefish were to translate what orange means to them, they'd all say 'Protein.'" Smethurst says. "I don't care if it's a marlin, milkfish, or whatever . . . orange is just one of those colors."

3. LITTLE GREEN MACHINE BY VINCE WILCOX, IDYLWILDE FLIES

Hook: Mustad 3906, #14-20
Head: Copper bead
Thread: 10/0 for #18-20, 8/0 for #14-16
Tail: Pheasant tail fiber tips
Rib: Ultrawire
Abdomen: Microtubing
Wing case: Pearl Fire-Fly
Gills: Antron fibers
Thorax: Ice Dub

Vince Wilcox

Little Green Machine.

Adirondacks-based fly tier Vince Wilcox has a talent for twisting up bugs that get the job done. His Little Green Machine (LGM) is no exception. Several years back on a Yampa River mission—the heavily-trafficked, often-times technical section below Stagecoach Reservoir—he plucked two #18 LGMs from his box, and dropped them into my cold, fishless hands. For the next several hours we found willing trout during an early spring snowstorm. I've since fished the LGM across the Front Range. And when things get stale and I'm struggling to find a micro-size pattern with the ability to produce amid multiple hatching insects, the versatile LGM stands out from the pack.

Wilcox designed the LGM. to imitate Baetis nymphs on Utah's Green River. But it's essentially a hybrid that covers both midges and Baetis, since the hatches often overlap. In addition, he uses the larger, full-dressed sizes for stillwaters to represent chironomids and callibaetis. The full flash back on the larger patterns delivers the "glowing" effect of a gassed-up emerger, while the wire rib shows segmentation and increases durability.

Wilcox says the LGM blueprint was derived as a meeting of three minds: Frank Sawyer's, Randall Kaufmann's, and his own. "Sawyer's Pheasant Tail nymph and perhaps the much lesser known Swannundaze Midges by Randall Kaufmann are excellent patterns in their own right," he says. "I think it's safe to say that Sawyer's Pheasant Tail inspired a great deal of the nymphs stocked in fly bins today and you would be hard pressed to find a fly shop that doesn't sell them. Kaufmann's Swannundaze Midge may not be in every fly shop, in fact it may not be in any, but that doesn't make it any less effective."

After mulling over the winning aspects of the Swannundaze, the PT, as well as his own VW Midge, Wilcox developed a hunch. "One of the things I have learned over thousands of days on the water and on the vise is that if you take nearly any Baetis imitation and shrink it down to a midge size, it's going to catch fish," he says. "The hybridization of these patterns as it evolved into the LGM proved successful due in part to that."

Wilcox substituted the traditional Pheasant Tail with tubing for an abdomen and Ice Dub for the thorax, creating a Baetis imitation that was effective and durable in smaller sizes. He then fused the front half of the VW Midge with the tail and straight shank hook from the modified Pheasant Tail. And he used gills instead of legs to give the fly more adaptability. Underwater looking up, trout see the LGM medley as a midge or Baetis but it's since gone one step further. As field tests progress we've also seen success with it as an impressionistic *Brachycentrus caddis*, or grannom.

"Since there are a great deal of bright green midge, caddis, and Baetis nymphs available in smaller sizes in moving water, my favorite color and size is chartreuse in size 18," Wilcox says. "Just compare the tiny chartreuse caddis larvae to the LGM and you will see they are very similar, in fact, almost a perfect match."

Because the LGM can be fished all season long through myriad hatch applications, this confidence fly remains a perennial answer to outthinking selective trout.

4. JUJUBAETIS BY CHARLIE CRAVEN, UMPQUA FLIES

Hook: TMC 2488, #16-22
Thread: White 10/0 for abdomen, Black 10/0 for thorax
Tail: Brown Hungarian partridge fibers
Abdomen: Two strands of brown Super Hair, one strand of black Super Hair.
Flash: Pearl Fire-Fly wingcase, grey Fluoro-Fiber thorax, black tying thread
Legs/Emergent wings: Leftover butts of Fluoro-Fiber wing case

Craven's Jujubaetis.

Charlie Craven, of Charlie's FlyBox in Arvada, Colorado, is one of the most talented fly tiers I've met, hands down. He has an irreverent sense of humor, skills that stem from years of busting out thousands of commercially tied patterns, and a substantial lineup of flies that are all business. For now, his highly effective Jujubaetis wears the crown, not only as a fish producer, but as a fly that's enamored fly fishers the world over in recent times.

The Jujubaetis was developed as an offshoot of Craven's original Jujubee Midge—a fly he'd been tweaking since the early '90s and that went into production at Umpqua in 1999.

"It was really just a variation of that," Craven says. "I'd been fishing it up in Cheesman Canyon alongside an RS2 and I'd catch just as many fish on it, so I figured they had to be eating it for a Baetis and that's what prompted me to add a tail."

The addition of the tail was the first in a series of modifications. Craven continued to tweak the pattern and submitted an updated version to Umpqua—sans epoxy overcoat—that never caught on. Back at the vise, he added a flash back to the fold and started experimenting with a palate of more exacting Baetis color schemes.

"I remember one day I was messing around with some leftover epoxy. I ran it over the head of a Jujubee Midge and as I did it the epoxy was kind of goobered up," Craven says. "Originally, I was just trying to do the wingcase but it ended up running down the length of the body."

Once the mistake solidified, Craven pondered the result and knew he was onto something. The addition of epoxy finished out the fly's silhouette, added durability, and imparted a perfect tear shape—much like a natural Baetis nymph. "This is what makes it stand out from other flies in the water," he says. "The silhouette is perfect—it's not *sort of*—it's exactly shaped like a Baetis nymph."

These first incarnations used Loon UV Knot Sense, but after repeated river use the coat would peel off. Craven currently uses Clear Cure Goo epoxy. He says it adds symmetry to the final product, blending the wingcase and thorax into one smooth unit. The fly has something else going for it, too: simplicity.

"The Barr Emerger is an example of a fly that is older than I am and still works as good as it ever did," Craven says. "It's simple like an RS2, a Hare's Ear, and a Pheasant Tail, and flies like that tend to last forever. The Jujubaetis is just a modernized version, but it still fits into that same mold."

The Jujubaetis has caught many a trout's eye in addition to those of fly fishers perusing shop bins for the latest greatest trout trap. It's Craven's best-selling pattern by a long shot. (In the last quarter prior to this writing Umpqua moved 1,800 dozen units of the Jujubaetis.) Color combinations run the gamut, from original brown to blues and purples and reds and a rusty-brown PMD version. Craven fishes blue and purple on overcast days and prefers it for tricking picky fish into charging at depth. As a general mayfly attractor pattern above and beyond its baetis duties, Craven has also added a 1.5 mm beaded version to the mix, which gives the fly enough weight to keep it down, in front of the fish.

Like the Pheasant Tails and Hare's Ears before it, the Jujubaetis has risen to the level of an "it" fly. Cinch one on your line and find out why.

5. GRAND MASTER FLASH BY ERIC ISHIWATA, IDYLWILDE FLIES

Hook: Any hook with 1.5-inch long shank
Thread: 8/0 Uni (wine)
Tag: Firewire loop, extended 1 inch past shank, 20lb mono loop half the length of Firewire
Butt: Med. Cactus Chenille (pearl), pheasant church window feather
Tail: 2 pairs ostrich at 10 and 2 (black)
Abdomen: Cream wool yarn
Thorax: Trout bead (any color)
Hackle: Whiting American Rooster Saddle (white dyed tan)
Flash: ~10-14 strands Flashabou (copper)
Wing: 6-8 strands ostrich herl (black)
Throat: 2 turns hen hackle (rust)
Horns: 2-inch long grizzly saddles tied at 10 and 2
Head: Hareline Pseudo Hair in dubbing loop (black)
Eyes: Med. Lead Dumbbells
Trailer: #6 Gamakatsu Octopus
Alternate color combos: 1. tan/gold, 2. olive/copper, and 3. black/blue

Photo by Geoff Mueller

Grand Master Flash.

Fort Collins-based fly tier Eric Ishiwata is a dedicated student of the swing, with a PhD honed under the tutelage of large and hard-to-catch trout of Wyoming's Miracle Mile system. His trout and steelhead streamers, built to excel with a traditional down-and-across wet-fly swing, have proved effective from Wyoming to Washington's Olympic Peninsula. And he has some solid thoughts on why.

I first met Eric, not in the river, but just outside Hannah, Wyoming, after I'd bottomed my truck out in a burly snowstorm en route to the Miracle Mile. My fishing partner and I had spent most of the morning hanging out in a ditch, until a local rancher mercifully freed us with a winch. Back on the road, Ishiwata and Jin Choi of St. Peter's Fly Shop were passing in the other direction and they waved us down to assess damages. Thankfully, all was intact other than the several hours of fishing we'd lost. This became even more evident by the shit-eating grins on our friends' wind-whipped faces.

"You guys nymph 'em up?" we asked. And a big "Nope!" was all we got as they continued on their merry way. Considering it was late January, we quickly crossed drys off the list, which logically led us to one single conclusion: swung streamers.

Along with the crew at St. Peter's—through tying demonstrations and on-the-water swing clinics—Ishiwata has been instrumental in enhancing the profile and use of steelhead techniques for duping Front Range trout. His ties are immaculate and meticulously engineered to the tune of how materials, alone and in various combinations, behave underwater. His basic design principles fall under four essential categories: size, profile, color, and flash.

"There are a couple of ways of thinking about fly size," Ishiwata says. "One is to consider the food sources in the system. If the river is loaded with 2-inch leeches and 3-inch sculpins, it makes sense to have your streamers follow suit." His other rule is to tie flies geared toward the fish you want to catch. "Flies should be large enough to eliminate dinks, yet reasonable enough to produce the kind of numbers you'd like." While swinging an 8-inch hunk of meat may eventually produce a trophy brown, the question is, *When*? In order to have the best odds for a "good" day, Ishiwata fishes a range of patterns between 2.5 and 4 inches long—although he's not opposed to chucking bigger bugs.

Over and above color, Ishiwata says profile is the single most important characteristic of swing-style flies. By profile, he's referring to the shape and movement the fly takes when pulled against the river's hydraulics.

"Too often, folks focus on how flies look in the vise or bins. While dead-drifted dries and nymphs undergo close inspection, making the case—perhaps—for anatomical correctness, and jerk-stripped articulates are built to trigger impulse reactions, swing-style flies swim across the river at a near-constant pace," he says. "I want my flies to replicate the profile and swimming movement of sculpins, crayfish, parr, and other baitfish. From a trout's-eye view—I suspect—a swinging streamer is more of a blur than a Quigley Cripple but less pandemonium than an Articulated Zoo Cougar."

Color is also critical. "There have been way too many times where a buddy and I have worked the same run, casting at similar angles, swinging at similar depths, and one of us was totally on the fish and the other completely off, with the only perceptible difference being the color of our flies," he says. Over the years, he's developed a handful of mini-theories (for instance, white/chartreuse for lake-run rainbows, black/copper for overcast skies, and olive/brown in the fall) that work as a general frame of reference. However, they've also been consistently debunked by obstinate trout. Therefore, Ishiwata ties all of his patterns in multiple color combinations—between three and seven schemes depending upon the pattern.

Last but not least is the element of flash. There was a period of time when Ishiwata only dabbled in natural materials. "I loved the classic aesthetics and bought in wholesale to legends like Rene Harrop who preach the superiority of CDC, marabou, and pheasant," he says.

"But I had too many days when Bubbas in blue jeans simply destroyed me using Mepps spinners. The reality is that there are times where loud and obnoxious flies outperform their drab cousins. Conversely, there are times where gaudy flies will absolutely turn trout off and this transition can take place from one hour to the next."

For now, Ishiwata continues to be inspired by everything from Spey-style PNW steelhead patterns to Chris Schrantz's deadly Platte River Spider. And translating anadromous-oriented concepts into flies such as his Grand Master Flash continues to produce slam-dunk swinging on Rocky Mountain freestone streams and tailwaters.

6. FILM CRITIC BY BOB QUIGLEY, IDYLWILDE FLIES

Like the Cripple, Bob Quigley's Film Critic was designed as a surface film pattern—what he called a floating half-submerger. Its stacked hackle suggests a struggling mayfly readying to buck its shuck and take flight.

Hook: Tiemco 2487 #10-12
Thread: Olive 8/0 UNI-Thread
Tail: Pheasant tail fibers
Rib: Copper wire
Abdomen: Pheasant tail fibers.
Wing: Z-Ion
Hackle: Saddle hackle, to match natural
Thorax: Olive superfine dubbing
Wing Buds: Z-Lon

Walk into any fly shop across the country. Step up to the assorted fly bins and home in on the mayfly dry selections. You'll find parachutes, winged CDCs, the standard stand-up hackles of traditional, Catskill-style mayfly duns and, typically, a handful of patterns that completely stand alone amidst the masses. These flies, with names such as Hackle Stacker, Loop Wing, Split Flag, Half Dun, and Film Critic, to the eye of the beholder, are more complex. They look difficult to tie, they incorporate nuances that the other drys fail to meet, and possess the modernisms of a mad scientist at the fly-tying vise. All these patterns have been conceptualized and brought to fruition by the late, great Bob Quigley.

Back in 1978, Quigley revolutionized the fly-fishing world when he birthed his Cripple pattern on the banks of California's Fall River. Through thousands of hours of observations on this technical spring creek, the Cripple was developed to mimic an emerging mayfly, one stuck in its shuck, with a trailing body that rode half-submerged in the water film. The pattern proved highly effective when pitted against that river's persnickety trout. It's since launched far past the Sunshine State as an essential fly for tough trout and, like many of Quigley's patterns, remains virtually unmatched in the realms of river-inspired technique and innovation.

The Cripple's distinctiveness stems from its forward cocked deer- or elk-hair wing, extending over the eye of the hook, with a butt section trimmed in line with a dubbed thorax. The rear portion of tail uses marabou tips. And the abdomen is spun marabou butts, twisted into a rope to represent the trailing shuck of a mayfly slipping free of its nymphal body. The half-in, half-out fly has since spawned many a copycat, but even in its original configuration it stands the test of time.

I first met Bob Quigley on a magazine assignment in southern Oregon, fishing the upper Williamson River. He was full of stories, many mind-blowing—ranging from exploits in Chile to his salad days raising hell in the Fall River Valley. Every evening, as we stepped off the river, Quigley returned to his desk for a maniacal fly-tying session, where he cranked out bizarro patterns. Some had massive rubber wings and foam abdomens, others had extended bodies with sexy pheasant tails demonstrating a perfect V split, while the drys we were fishing had expertly spun hackled heads. What they all shared in common was their nuanced differences, a Quigley signature. Bob Quigley was known to never tie the same fly twice. When we brought them back out on the river to test, they each produced in their own way.

Fly tier Kenny Morrish has been a Bob Quigley fan and follower since long before the two ever met. He became acquainted with the name behind the brash patterns as an impressionable eleven-year-old perusing the San Mateo fly-fishing show.

"I walked into a booth and one of the tiers whipped out this fly. It was an incredible Matuka sculpin with a mixed-dyed cree back, immaculate ribbing, and it had this multi-colored deer-hair head," Morrish says. "It had spots on it and it was trimmed up like a triceratops. Right on the front of the sculpin, he'd tied a glo-bug."

The fly would be the precursor to the egg-sucking-style patterns that are now standard trout and steelhead producers. Morrish was impressed, and when he asked who tied it, the name behind the outlandish bug was, of course, Bob Quigley. Years later, Morrish began fishing Quigley's early dry-fly iterations on rivers such as the Fall and Hat Creek. One such pattern—the Cripple—he says completely changed his fishing experience for the better.

A trout bum before the concept was ever coined and commercialized, Quigley spent his days living for the next trout or steelhead. He never owned a car, lived in fly-shop attics, trailers, and the back of a van for a while, all the while trailblazing new fly-tying techniques. Quigley didn't borrow much off others. He was a true innovator.

What drove that innovation was keen observation skills. Quigley had plenty of time on the water—more than most—and he wasn't anxious or hurried about the process. He also had a world-class testing ground in the form of the Fall River to bounce ideas off. He possessed a scientific eye to understand why things were and weren't working. And he combined that with a tinkering desire to tweak and make flies better.

"The combination of inspiration and the proper substances is a great path," Morrish says. "I still think his classic Cripple was the greatest game changer—this marabou-backed Quigley Cripple has proven to be a super-important fly."

Quigley passed away in June 2012 after a battle with prostate cancer. His interpretive flies continue to transcend space and time.

. . . .

In addition to the above-mentioned standouts and their corresponding stories, there is more to fly selection than just choosing a bug by a famous tier who gave it a fancy name. Fly selection is based on myriad on- and under-the-water observations that oftentimes start with a hatch and are followed by our attempts to replicate it. Ishiwata tells us about color and profile, Conaty talks about getting lucky by tweaking materials into a fly recipe trout find irresistible, while Quigley took what he knew about dry-fly fishing and enhanced it through technique and inspired engineering.

There are plenty of flies out there that fall into these categories. John Barr's Copper John, for instance, came as a result of the hopper-dropper technique pioneered by Colorado's Jackson Streit. Barr developed the fly on the premise that a rapidly sinking bug would get to the fish faster when fishing short rigs under a hopper. The Copper John, with its wire-ribbed body and epoxy-flash back, was also designed as an attractor to focus a trout's attention toward a "real fly," such as an emerger or pupa, riding below it. After several years of field-testing it in the '90s, Barr changed hooks and materials and the Copper John was a finished product. To Barr's surprise, it turned out to be an effective fly on its own, as well as performing in its intended bait-and-switch role.

The Copper John mimics a mayfly silhouette beautifully and is available in a full spectrum of colors and variations on the shelf. I always keep a loaded row of blues in my arsenal because it's proven to be the most effective color for me on big Western tailwaters, where trout seem to focus in on a highly specific color spectrum—one that we can't see. The fly inspires confidence in that specific color because I fish it, and it works. And whatever flies we choose to make up our confidence boxes, our decisions should be based on logic. Fly tiers spend years developing these patterns to get them just right. Even standard bugs on shop shelves are mostly in a constant state of change. Specific watersheds, such as headwaters, tailwaters, or spring creeks, their hatches (and non-hatches), and the available trout species and their varying habitats all help determine how well our flies will perform. Experimentation leads us down the path to success more often than not. Had I never fished a Copper John in blue, I may have missed some great trout.

And with that said, maybe it's time to tie on Coach Knight's TeQueely. . . because even the most tried-and-tested confidence flies need a shake-up now and again.

10 Connecting the D.O.T.S

On the following page I unveil the peerless techniques that I employed in order to catch enough fish to prevent the raging floodwaters from topping the levees at Lizard Bend Montana.

—Sheridan Anderson, *The Curtis Creek Manifesto*

When Tim Romano and I first embarked on this project the goal was to enlighten our fly-fishing minds by diving into a trout's underexplored environment. By learning first-hand how and where trout live, behave, see, and use their various senses in their natural habitats, the hope was to resurface with applicable fly-fishing beta—to unlock the vault and resurface with a pile of secrets. And our angling know-how has benefitted from the journey.

The quirky world of trout will always remain somewhat subjective because the way trout process information differs from the way we do. Regardless, investigative fly fishers through lifetimes of trial and error have made good progress in this realm. From Bob Nastasi and Al Caucci to Sheridan Anderson, Gary LaFontaine, Robert Behnke, and Ernest Schwiebert, to contemporary explorers such as Brian Chan and Ralph Cutter, our knowledge of trout behavior and how it pertains to fly-fishing success has grown exponentially. By donning mask and snorkel and dunking our heads underwater, we too have become that much more intimate with our quarry—and what we're seeing underwater is a shifting picture of

Habitat is essential to trout-feeding behavior. Understanding it helps us better decipher where trout live and how to best target them.

environments in a state of flux. The underwater world is not static and trout, being expert adapters, are constantly forced to alter their routines to survive and thrive. Habitat to a large degree, dictates behavior, and understanding how it plays into trout feeding behavior is key to becoming better anglers.

Trout are instinctual creatures, and one of the most surprising realizations to stem from this research is their inability to fully comprehend what *we* mean to *them* as awkwardly swimming earthlings. Trout spook from above as part of a predator-prey response sparked by everything from the overhead swoop of a wing to the spray of an errant cast to the reverberations we send into the water by stepping too close to the riverbank. Our mistakes above the water are evident and easily identifiable. What's remarkable, however, is the tolerance trout show to a couple of 170-pound dudes—bedecked in full snorkeling gear—hovering above, beside, and below them. Clearly, trout have not generated much of an adaptive response to those of us intent on watching and studying them, as opposed to catching them.

When fisheries biologist John McMillan goes underwater and tempts a steelhead with a couple of feet of Maxima and a swung fly protruding off his finger, the fish eats—despite his presence. This is good news for fly fishers: the fact that fish are more concerned with eating, as it pertains to survival, than they often are with you and me. Fish are generally hyper-focused on food, with ambitions to grow big and strong and mate to maintain the next generation. And for that, they will continually be focused on our flies.

It's a fascinating world under the surface film, where we've gained insights on everything from when, where, and why trout feed to how they perceive and react to our presentations delivered from above. We've learned how trout vision plays into fly selection, how metabolic function forces seasonal behavioral changes, and how trout have evolved, and continue to evolve, to many of the contemporary realities at play. Tailwater trout are different than freestone trout in that their habitats dictate a string of varying behaviors during the year. Native and wild trout are different than stocker breeds in their abilities to better perceive home and react accordingly to the threats at play. Different species of trout, from rainbows to browns to cutthroat to brookies to hybrids incubated in hatchery holding cells, all present unique challenges when it comes to our fishing game. From underwater looking up, here are a few tips on how to hone it.

WHAT TROUT SEE—HABITAT

One of the driving forces behind these pages is seeing the river through the trout's unblinking eye and applying that view to our fishing. From a fly-fishing perspective, there are several ways to look at how trout see and engage in their underwater environs. First, when it comes to finding fish, it's imperative to know what cornerstones signify ideal trout habitat. By understanding where trout lie during prime feeding events, less time is wasted hammering subpar water, and we can focus more effort on distinct river sections that consistently produce results.

In order to see and comprehend rivers through a trout's unblinking eye, it pays to put your head underwater. Cobblestone bottom, somewhere deep within Washington's Olympic National Park.

When trout swim a river, they are looking for several key ingredients—underwater nuances that drive overall health. Where and when a trout decides to park and dine can be broken down by specific areas that offer respite in the form of obstructed and oxygenated flows, cover in the form of overhead and underwater structure, feeding lanes in the form of areas where food availability is high, and areas that offer temperature relief—from extreme highs and lows—through variables such as depth, under-water springs, and tributary confluences. Productive trout streams have some or all of these elements throughout their courses. The more nuanced a river, with uninhibited freedom for fish to move from one habitat preference to the next, the better off those trout populations are.

When examining a river through human eyes, it's important to recognize how hydraulics are affected by in-stream structure, and how those bends, funnels, drops, twists, turns, banks, and speed bumps pertain to a stationary, feeding trout, or a cruiser in search of a big gulp. As far as feeding is concerned, the river is a move-able feast (thank you, Hemingway). And breaking down its basic course into easily digestible segments is the first step to sourcing more fish . . . more of the time.

1. Fish the fast stuff

Trout source riffles because these shallow, fast-flowing segments produce oxygenated water—away from more stagnant areas, where heat intensifies during low-flow summer doldrums. Riffles are also one of the—if not *the*—most productive areas for aquatic insects such as may-flies and caddis to develop underwater and pop skyward as adults. During heavy hatches, take the time to observe riffle areas. Although it's easier to spot a solitary riser in the slicks and seams below and above the chop, by studying riffles closely you'll identify surface takes there, too. The obvious advantage of fishing riffle water is that the faster flows limit a trout's window to inspect and

Shallow, fast-flowing riffles provide temperature reprieve for trout and are productive areas to source hatch activity.

potentially snub your bug. Instead, trout react quickly amid the chaos. Riffles present good opportunities to cover water and when the surface take is slow, when trout are focused head-down on nymphs and emergers, you can still effectively dupe fish in the shallows with dry-dropper rigs, or by using a small, light strike indicator, such as yarn. In skinny water nymphing scenarios, drift your bugs mid to low in the water column and be prepared to strike fast. When fishing water less than 3 feet deep, skip the heavier BB shot and drop down to No. 4s or lose the split-shot entirely and stick with a beadhead fished off the bend of an unweighted fly to move your presentation into the preferred depth zone.

2. Pools are a must-hit

Pools provide the deepest holding areas in a river and are easily identifiable as the slow-moving sections where faster currents collide into a broad, slow-moving belly. Pools hold trout during much of the day, as well as times of the year when flows drop and trout seek refuge against extreme temps on both sides of the thermometer. This deeper, darker water has ample overhead cover, protecting submarining trout from predators. And as winter moves in and trout metabolism slows, they hold in these areas, avoiding shallower sections that may be prone to anchor ice, for instance, and thus less productive.

The US Fish & Wildlife Service defines optimal pool habitat as having the depth, size, and low-flow velocities needed to sustain several resting adult trout. But in addition to restoring energy, trout feed in pools, too. Fishing larger pools has limitations, especially when it comes to delivering optimal drag-free drifts. For instance, currents in pools tend to oscillate—often due to a fast seam in the center, where a riffle enters. This faster water eventually hits the brakes when it collides into the slower-moving pool core. At this point, it is deflected to either side— left and right—creating eddies that move back upstream, along its peripheries, toward the pool head. In order to effectively fish pools, a thorough read of its haphazard currents is paramount.

If the river flows downstream in the center and upstream along the banks, trout can be found facing and feeding in multiple directions in a single pool. Knowing which direction they are looking allows you to feed the fish via both dry-fly and nymphing presentations. Optimal positioning within the pool, from upstream into the heavier flow and from downstream and across into the trickier side currents is your best blueprint for covering this water. Mending is also an essential element to the game, especially when fishing across side-eddies into the faster center flow. The key is to make sure your fly line is moving in the same direction as the current. For example, if an upstream current is fighting your downstream drift, stack mend (explained below) downstream to keep your presentation moving toward your target.

3. The run of the river

Runs—or glides and flats—can be defined as the transitional areas located below pools and above riffles. And these meaty, intermediary sections can offer the best of both worlds when it comes to trout habitat. Runs provide trout with diversity: space to rest, feed, and roam when their daily habitat requirements change. Trout also seek runs during hatch events because they offer consistencies, such as sufficient depth for overhead cover, a walking-pace speed that requires less energy expenditure, and long, unrestricted lanes that channel high volumes of food.

These areas, which can exist for seemingly miles on prime dry-fly waters such as the Railroad Ranch section of the Henry's Fork, are tops when fish are looking up. Unlike riffles, however, expect that your flies and presentations have ample time to be investigated by trout keyed in on specific insect nuances—size, color, stage, and behavior in the water. With those elements in mind, these technical stretches require precision reading by fly fishers intent on hitting their mark. If there was ever a river section you wanted to stop on the bank and sit and contemplate the situation of a rising trout—taking a long swig of something brown and mulling it over—this is it.

Run-oriented trout, holding in a couple of feet of steady-paced water and making the smallest dimple on the river's surface during an autumn trico hatch, are oftentimes some of the biggest, baddest specimens in Trout Town. They're there with two wants in mind: 1) to avoid a hook, and 2) to sit and hoover down bugs until their guts are stuffed. Presentation often requires longer casts, on longer leaders and thinner tippets to take into account microdrag on the river's surface. The key is to make a delivery—no more than 3 feet for accuracy purposes—upstream of your intended quarry. And you want the fish to see your fly, and nothing else. This water type is renowned for putting human error under a microscope, so make first casts count. (You may not get a second chance in Last Chance, Idaho.) Wade carefully, and thoughtfully. From downstream, you can potentially wade closer to a feeding fish without spooking it. From upstream and across, you have the best chance at making a clean, fly-first delivery. Lastly, pay ultraclose attention to the feeding cadence of your intended target. Observe, quietly, count the seconds between each rise, and time your casts accordingly. You want your fly to be in full view when the trout moves in for the kill.

Trout are generally looking for opportunity. By understanding the basics of riffles, pools, and runs, your chances to intercept them increase—especially on large rivers where you are covering substantial amounts of water. Knowing which rigs to fish—and when—is the next step to deciphering what a trout *wants* to see and how to deliver that to them effectively.

WHAT TROUT SEE—RIGS

A common mistake I see on the water are rigs that make no sense. We know that trout feeding behavior is largely influenced by what's going on under the water. Trout feed in areas that offer a breather from ripping currents, where bugs congregate en masse, and in areas where they feel generally protected from overhead predation. Once they've found their preferred cafeteria lineup, their feeding behavior undergoes a secondary set of criteria based on what's hatching, and where it is predominating in the water column. Deciphering whether or not trout are scouring the river bottom for nymphs, are elevated in the mid-water column and hammering emergers, or are surface prone—looking for stuck-in-the-shuck cripples or adults—are the first considerations that lead us toward choosing proper rigs.

On a recent trip to a favorite Wyoming tailwater my fishing buddy and I woke up from our tents to the rock-and-roll sounds of cicadas strumming their "tymbals" on the sides of their abdominal base. We'd heard secondhand reports of the event and we'd shown up with piles of Chubby Chernobyls and a black Sharpie Marker to "match the hatch." Cicadas, according to our good friends at Wikipedia, have long been considered fine dining by people around the world, including those in Ancient Greece, as well as China, Malaysia, Burma, Latin America, and the Congo. It's also a well-known fact that their occurrence on the river, often cyclical in nature, is prized by large trout that lose all sense of inhibition when the meaty, translucent winged bugs plop anywhere near their range of view. That day, nearly every damn fish we presented with our doctored Chubbys moved—anywhere from 6 inches to 6 feet—to absolutely annihilate our flies. Cicadas, where you can find them, present one of the best dry-fly fishing opportunities for big fish you will experience across the country. And somehow, we'd lucked into the melee.

The rig for throwing a big dry fly to big fish is a relatively simple one. We fished 8- to 12-pound tippets, double-surgeon knotted to stout leaders in the 9-foot range. A no brainer. The fish weren't tippet shy, and they were eating on top. But during all this activity over our two-day stay in cicada heaven, we couldn't help but notice the poor fools dredging the other side of the river with tandem-fly nymph rigs and seemingly having little luck. They'd picked up a fish or two here and there, but they were definitely fishing the wrong rig during the right hatch. Clearly, they hadn't received the memo.

To the credit of the dudes across the way, cicada hatches—without some astute observations, or a phone call from someone in the know—can be easy to miss. Like October Caddis and some Golden Stone events, and unlike blanket mayfly hatches, they are less obvious to the casual observer. But trout key on these big protein emergences and whether or not they are evident on the water, you want to look for other clues that indicate their presence. (The chorus emanating from the bankside, for instance.) Moreover, there's a lesson here when it comes to rigging: 1) keen observation of what's happening in the riparian corridor is often just as essential as what's taking place on the water, and 2) you will have the best success using an appropriate rig that produces what trout want to see.

Proper rigging is one of the most daunting tasks for rookie fly fishers. There are knots involved, sometimes many, and when it comes to subsurface presentations there can be multiple flies connected to multiple tippets, adorned with multiple bells and whistles including split-shots and strike indicators floating the whole mess up- or downstream. These more elaborate rigs present many opportunities to whip and cast the whole Christmas tree into a knotted pile of ineffectualness at the end of your line. With that in mind, the most important rigging lesson is perhaps to keep things as simple as possible.

Fly-fishing expert Charles Meck is a rigging master and his book, *Fishing Tandem Flies,* is a great primer to all the rigs you'd ever need to catch a plethora of trout from Lees Ferry in Colorado to the technical spring creeks of Pennsylvania's State College area. Meck writes: "Fishing a combination of dry flies and nymphs or more than one subsurface pattern—also called a tandem rig—is one of the simplest, most effective ways to fish . . . A lot of skilled fly fishers intensely watch the end of their fly lines, or strike indicators, waiting for the first indication of a strike so they can quickly set the hook. I can't bear this for long. With a tandem rig, I could watch a dry fly, which for me is a more exciting and interesting way to

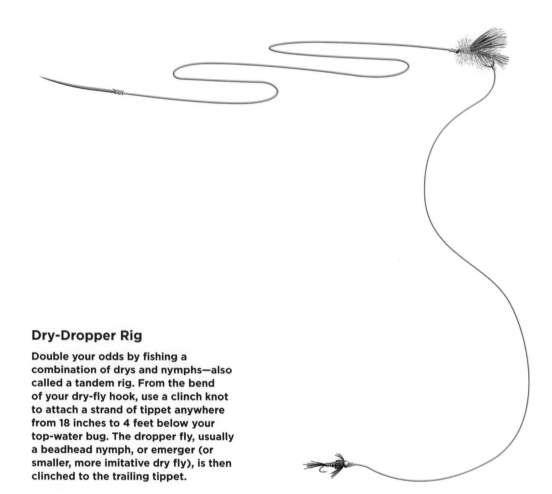

Dry-Dropper Rig

Double your odds by fishing a combination of drys and nymphs—also called a tandem rig. From the bend of your dry-fly hook, use a clinch knot to attach a strand of tippet anywhere from 18 inches to 4 feet below your top-water bug. The dropper fly, usually a beadhead nymph, or emerger (or smaller, more imitative dry fly), is then clinched to the trailing tippet.

fish a nymph. Also, the fortuitous strikes on the dry fly that I would never have had give me great delight."

What Meck is describing is essentially the "dry-dropper" rig, and it's about as basic a dry-nymph setup you could bring to the trout table. It involves a single, unsinkable battleship—anything from the Chubby mentioned above to a large Parachute Adams, Trude, or Wulff variation. From the bend of your dry-fly hook, use a

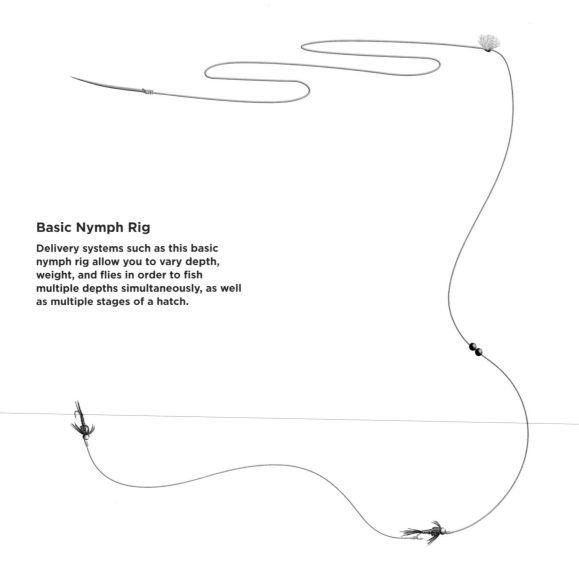

Basic Nymph Rig

Delivery systems such as this basic nymph rig allow you to vary depth, weight, and flies in order to fish multiple depths simultaneously, as well as multiple stages of a hatch.

clinch knot to attach a strand of tippet, anywhere from 18 inches to 4 feet below your top-water bug. The dropper fly, usually a beadhead nymph, or emerger (or smaller, more imitative dry fly), is then clinched to the trailing tippet. Voila, with the dry-dropper you are stoning many birds with one hit. The advantages are several: For one, you can easily spot your larger, topwater attractor fly, which acts as an indicator with hooking potential. Second, unlike heavier and longer split-shot bedecked rigs, this combination lands softly allowing you to still target trout in skinnier water. Your dropper options are endless, from exacting, anatomically correct subsurface imitations placed at precision depths to floating meatier nymphs such as a Pat's Rubber Legs, 20 Inchers, or Princes. And last, if the trout wants your top bug over the bottom selection, you're still in the game. Dry-dropper disadvantages stem from the need to fish deeper and in instances that call for heavy-water presentations. This rig is not suited for deep dredging. And when multiple-fly combinations and heavy weight are required, your dry needs to be buoyant enough to shoulder the load. When it's not, it's time to lose it and switch to a new tactic.

Deep-water nymphing calls for more complicated rigging options and, to avoid cursed windknots and wasted time re-rigging, less false casting is key. My basic nymph rig—from top to bottom—consists of a strike indicator (usually yarn), split-shot or non-toxic tungsten putty, and two flies. The strike indicator allows you to control top-to-bottom depth, while the split-shot gets you into the zone faster—and keeps you there longer. As a general rule, the distance between indicator and your bottom fly should be about one-and-a-half times the river depth. Factors such as water type, slow or fast, and what stage of insect emergence trout are keyed in on all play into the indictor placement equation. Basically, if every other cast results in a snag, move your strike indicator down to raise your rig. Your split-shot rests at the leader tippet junction. And I like to keep the distance between weight and top fly relatively tight, no more than 6 inches to maintain the connection as close to inline as possible when it's drifting through holding water. The top fly is clinched to the tippet and I drop bottom flies approximately 8 inches off the hook bend with another strand of tippet. The beauty of this rig is that with two or more flies, the experimentation potential is endless. Not only can you fish multiple depths at the same time, but you can also fish multiple stages of a hatch, for instance with a Baetis nymph on the bottom and a gilled emerger riding higher in the water column.

A simple, functioning nymph rig increases your odds when fishing subsurface and there are many variations out there. Trout have seen them all at one time or another, and we know they see them well. Tippets and leaders, no matter what the size—and despite what some manufacturers will tell you—reflect light brilliantly underwater. Even split-shot, more often than you might think, is sampled by curious, bottom-grubbing trout. Although this might seem to defeat the intended purpose, more often than not, trout still bite the fly drifting from the business end of your rig. Good rigging increases these opportunities, but it is pointless, quite literally, without succinct delivery methods. If there's anything that's been beaten over our heads through thousands of hours of underwater observations it's that presentation counts—and when you screw it up, trout notice.

WHAT TROUT SEE—PRESENTATIONS

PhDs in space-age rigging systems, knowledge of ancient river methodologies, possession of high-tech gadgetry, and a one-way ticket to the most trout-choked waters on Planet Earth are no guarantees to going skunk free. They may help, but they are often rendered useless by piss-poor technique. Delivering your fly to trout, in a natural manner that doesn't send scare-signals to an instinctually honed brain, is the crux of Mount Flyfishing. To make better presentations, acquainting oneself with a trout's wants and desires is the first sure-fire step to victory.

Trout positioned in the water column, with the intent to feed, are happy trout. They are situated here—riffle, run, pool, behind or in front of a boulder, buried deep under a rip-rock bank, ready to smash—at this particular time, for several reasons. The main one being the opportunity to stop, gulp, swallow, and absorb the calories that fuel their quest to move through life phases and eventually produce the next year's class. Trout are keen eaters and this fact drives their underwater behaviors all season long.

Now that we've identified the where, in addition to the rigs needed to get the job done, the next consideration is how to best serve our flies. This is where casts, and how they pertain to presentation, come into play. We know that trout often feed in a stationary matter. Hydraulic force and the currents that crisscross a river's path, on the other hand, act as a conveyor belt shuffling protein from upstream to down so it can be intercepted while en route. When mayfly nymphs, for instance, are released from the river cobble and begin the migration from bottom to top, they are picked up in the vortex and move in a natural drift trout are used to seeing. They also buck, undulate, and swim, but they do not *drag* because they're unattached to anything—other than velocity. Flies, in their natural state, move to the tune of the river. Good presentations do the same.

Back when fly fishing was purely a "gentleman's" sport—long before high- and low-holing trout bums polluted the mix—the upstream, dry-fly cast was *the* acceptable method. And those traditionalists, despite their tweed-wearing ways, were definitely on to something. An upstream cast, either straight ahead or quartered above and to either side of a trout, delivers a stationary fly that, once it hits the water, moves downstream in unison with your fly line and preferred choice of rigs. When done right, the whole ensemble travels at the same speed of the current and trout react to these presentations favorably. In addition to fishing drys, the upstream presentation is equally effective for nymphs. By casting well upstream of your target, a nymph rig has time to straighten out and settle to a desired depth. Line control is important: you want to strip in any fly line slack quickly, to keep pace with the drift. A tight connection is key, so when the trout hits, indicated by your indicator stalling, wiggling, or plummeting into the river, you can lift your rod simultaneously to set the hook. From underwater looking up, trout sample, taste, and spit out constantly. In clear water, sight-fishing scenarios, you should be able to spot a trout as it inhales your bug. Telltale signs include the flash of its side as it turns on your fly or a brief wink of white produced by the opening of its mouth. With a trained eye and wicked reflexes, you can even ditch the indicator entirely, which will no doubt make the traditionalists snort and applaud with small golf claps.

Plotting presentations. The author (left) and Seattle-area guide Dave McCoy stand at the head of a broad plunge pool, where divergent currents can make assessing the best-cast-scenario complicated.

In addition to the upstream techniques of old, there has been marked progression on the water over the past hundred or so years. We no longer solely fish *up* and much of our fishing and what we know about trout behavior has added new presentations to the arsenal. For instance, rivers present many cases where a straight upstream cast is either not possible—due to obstructions or dicey wading—or just plain ineffectual when it comes to getting your fly in front of a trout. When you flip the traditional on its head, downstream and across is what you're left with. For fishing dry flies, this may seem counterintuitive. By landing a dry fly downstream, into a current that is also moving downstream, it is quicker to catch drag. The same goes for a nymph rig. But being such a savvy bunch, contemporary fly fishers have developed a remedy to help eliminate this effect and expand the gape of the downstream, drag-free window. The technique is called, wait for it . . . *mending.*

Mending is a repositioning of your fly line—typically the belly as it floats across the current—in an upstream sweep off and back onto the water. When done right, it defeats the divergent current speeds between you and a trout, allowing for a drag-free drift.

Mending is essentially a repositioning of your fly line—typically the belly as it floats across the current—in an upstream sweep off and back onto the water. When done right, it defeats the divergent current speeds between you and a trout. Water near the riverbank, for instance, runs slower than that pushing through the middle of a run. The upstream mend counters those differences in pace. Keep in mind that whether nymphing or throwing drys, you want to lift (mend) your line deftly, without moving your leader and tippet and fly, which could send a trout packing. Aerial mends and stack mends are two variations on the theme. The aerial mend, true to its name, is conducted in the air, before your presentation drops to the river's surface. Simply reach with your rod—arm across your body—in an upstream motion as your line unfurls down and across the river. When timed right, everything lands upstream, allowing for a clean, elongated downstream drift. The stack mend is the pluralized version of the original mend. It's best for fishing to trout positioned well downstream and it involves placing simultaneous mends on top of each other—stacked upstream—to run as long a drift as possible through good holding water. Line control here is also essential, as you'll have a lot of it out on the water. The technique also calls for an exaggerated set to drive the hook home.

Because trout are more often than not counterintuitive creatures, there are, of course, exceptions to presentation rules. For instance, and to make things more confusing, there are times on the water when a dead drifted fly is a little too stilted. If you've ever experienced a heavy Western green drake hatch, you know these supercharged mayflies, as adults, are about as animated as it gets. The river flows downstream and they bounce, crash, and catapult up it. Caddis, also, are highly active. The pupae swim fast and you'll often see trout explode through the river's surface to whale a bug in midair. Several innovative fly fishers of Pacific Northwest steelhead fame, such as Ed Ward and Scott Howell, have helped drive skating or waking-fly techniques to the surface, so to speak. Wet and dry-fly swinging techniques, although not new by any means, are designed to instigate a trout's predatory response through moving, breathing, gurgling, and undulating presentations that use currents to give flies added life. Nymphs and midges, too, are astir and move in the water column, and strikes can often occur at the end of a dead drift, while your presentation is ascending—much like a naturally hatching fly. It pays to be patient and fish through the swing. A live mouse swims for its life when it hits the water in brown trout territory. Your presentation should be equally alive, when the situation calls for it.

Last, the presentations outlined here involve a certain degree of accuracy and skill. Sure, plenty of fly fishers can barely cast their way out of their girlfriend's handbag and still catch fish. But I guarantee those with casting marksmanship, who can throw a tight-looped double-haul through a wall of wind, in addition to a bank-side underhand cast through a needle-eye of sticky thickets, have a significant advantage—anywhere they fish. Practice your presentations, and practice them often, because unforgiving trout are on constant high alert for deliveries that don't quite look right.

WHAT TROUT SEE—COLOR, SIZE, AND PROFILE

There is no shortage of color talk contained within these pages. We know trout pay laser-sharp attention to it, and so should you. And now that you have prime lies, rigs, and presentations already on the brain, the next step is choosing the right bug for the right time to get the job done. A key consideration when it comes to what trout see is color. Trout see colors accurately, but differently than us. They have the ability to discern between infrared

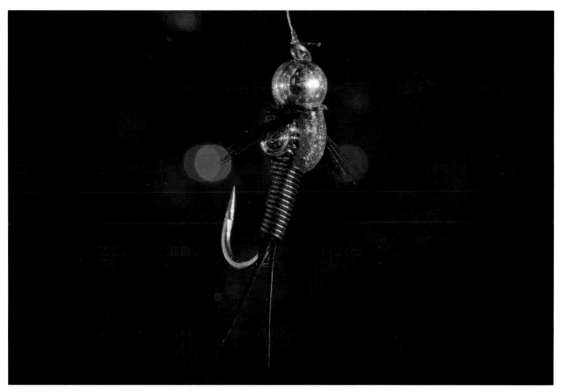

The success of purple and blue patterns—such as the blue Copper John, here—has sparked revolutionary results on the river. In addition to color a trout's eye is also highly capable of detecting size, profile, silhouette, and motion.

and UV light, which the human eye can't. And below the surface, the colors we've worked so hard to accurately mimic change drastically due to everything from in-the-river characteristics, such as siltation load and overall clarity, to the effects of depth in relation to light lost or gained. All these factors bend and mute color, adding another significant element to our fly-box selection process. The old swear-by to "match the color of the predominant hatch" has, to a large degree, been blow out of the water in recent times. Some experts suggest mixing as many colors of the rainbow as possible into one single fly, in the hopes you might get something right. Others say, pay less attention to color and focus your efforts on shape, profile, and silhouette. We'll discuss both sides of the coin, but let's start with the standalones.

Colors that have intrigued me most in recent times, and seem to have the same effect on trout, are those that fall into the purple and blue end of the spectrum. Prince may have popularized *Purple Rain* waaay back in the '80s but it's been contemporary Rocky Mountain guides singing the virtues of purple Prince nymphs, Poison Tungs, Purple Hazes, Purple Renegades, and purple and blue worms that have sparked a new revolution on the water. On a recent spring trip to the Missouri with the crew at Headhunters Fly Shop out of Craig, Montana, we experimented with purple Cripples in addition to standard hatch-matching colors during a Baetis storm that brought the river to a froth with rising trout. When the weather turned overcast in the late afternoon, our little purple pills proved far more intoxicating to trout than their more exacting-colored counterparts. Colorado fly-tying wizard Charlie Craven confirms that he also does best with his killer purple Jujubaetis nymphs under a gray sky that draws unseen characteristics out of patterns that trout find irresistible.

North Platte Lodge/Reef Fly Shop guide Stu Birdsong tells us of the phenomenal success he's had experimenting with purple and blue patterns—in particular the worm. His clients hook hundreds of sizeable browns and rainbows on the Grey Reef section of the North Platte River and on other prime Wyoming tailwaters with them annually. In the river and under the water, he's tested it against chartreuse, pinks, and reds, and his findings are striking: Purple continues to produce over and above other color options. Birdsong attributes the phenomenon to underwater characteristics, rather than low-light scenarios which seem to drive the success of purple and blue dries. The Reef runs with a high sediment load through most of the season. Water clarity, although good, is highly different than the streak-free glass view you see on other tailwaters such as the Missouri and Green. He says when purple is viewed against brownish or tannin-colored water, it takes on a more natural light, in addition to having more "pop" or "stage presence" than the traditional colors of flies past.

What's apparent is that what we're seeing as far as color is oftentimes nowhere near what trout are experiencing. What human eyes perceive as green, for instance, is made up of reflections of blues and yellows. Add infrared and ultraviolet to the mix and the idea of standard "green" becomes even splotchier. The idea and practice of fishing purples and blues has added some clarity to the conundrum. We might not be able to comprehend exactly why it works. But the fact that trout like it is sometimes answer enough.

In addition to tinkering with colors in the blue and purple end of the spectrum, Kirk Deeter, author of *The Little Red Book of Fly Fishing,* has written extensively about the use of "hot spots" or "trigger points" on fly patterns. He says that adding fluorescent material accents in key places like the collar or tail of a beadhead nymph, creates focal points that trout may see better, and react favorably to. In attempts to bridge the gap between what fly fishers see and what trout see, Deeter has spent a lot of time scuba diving rivers, and has been struck by how much color changes as natural light penetration through the water decreases. He says, "That hot pink San Juan worm doesn't look all that hot 10 feet below the lake surface (it looks grey), especially when there's a lot of particulate matter suspended in the water. The less light penetration, the more you lose the reds, and the better you see yellows, for example. And blues maintain a solid silhouette."

Although it's somewhat speculative, it can be assumed that the effect is similar in the eyes of a trout. Deeter says he's never seen anything natural that looks anything like a purple Prince nymph. "But the way that color acts in the light environment of a river is its real appeal."

In addition to color a trout's eye is also highly capable of detecting size, profile, silhouette, and motion. As we fish deeper into the river or lake abyss, these attributes become more and more prevalent. Fort Collins-based fly tier, Eric Ishiwata, says profile—or the shape and movement the fly takes when pulled against the river's hydraulics—is one of the most important characteristic to triggering positive trout responses. When building and fishing his swing-style flies, Ishiwata pays close attention to how they move under tension. Fishing teardrop-shaped patterns animated by soft-flowing materials that move toward the rear of the fly is the basic formula for achieving this effect. "It's the same principle behind a Lady Caroline, Akroyd, Tube Snake, Intruder, and Prom Dress," he says. "The key is to source patterns with stiff or bulky materials in front of or directly behind softer fibers that avoid compression and maintain a lifelike presentation." These flies, when brought into the underwater fold, and are then swung under tension against or parallel to downstream currents, effectively do a lot of the work for you. The trout sees a living, breathing entity scurrying into and back out of its feeding zone. When a predatory response is sparked, the chase is on.

Similar to the swung bug, strip-and-jerk techniques used effectively by streamer-heads such as Kelly Galloup, on the Madison, and Doug McKnight, on the Yellowstone, streamers are designed to incite motion in accordance with a trout's instinctual, pull-the-trigger-and-bite reaction. McKnight's Home Invader patterns came to life in 1995 as a direct result of "matching the minnow hatch" on a small spring creek. Since then, it's produced many an oversize brown on McKnight's home waters in and around Livingston, Montana. Shape and action are the main reason these flies work so well. "What I came up with was a lively little streamer made of rooster hackles, marabou, fur, lead eyes, and some flash," the designer says. "When wet, the materials slick up and turn into a perfect minnow shape, and it becomes alive in the water." McKnight's streamer program is an intense one.

It involves throwing 8-weights, with heavy 300-grain sinking-heads. He typically fishes two flies in unison, and fishes them big. This limits smaller fish from the catching mix, focusing on large, territorial predators in deep lairs. Flies are thrown from a moving drift boat toward the bank, and the retrieve, depending on water depth, begins the instant the Home Invader hits the water. Heavy lead eyes give the pattern an up-and-down jigging motion with each pull, and the goal is to keep it active.

The ability to synchronize fundamental elements (such as habitat identification, rig construction, line techniques, and fly selection) is essential to developing an underwater-achiever skillset. Fully understanding what trout see can be a murky proposition, but with an open mind to artistic interpretation and tuned tools the picture starts to make sense. What's absolutely clear is the fact that trout notice everything—from our mistakes to our successes (both intended and accidental). Will the human mind ever actually be able to fully comprehend a trout's frame of vision? Probably not; Our goggles are just wired differently. But the more we can think in parallel to their experience, the better anglers we become.

11 Threats: You, Me, and Maintaining Wildness within the Bubble

Remember, no man ever caught a trout in a dirty place.

—Robert B. Roosevelt, America's piscicultural "high priest"

If the trout are lost, smash the state.

—Thomas McGuane

From outside looking in, trout exist in a bubble. When the framework that houses their happy little existence cracks, it takes more than Band-Aids to fix it. And when the bleeding starts, one common abuser is to blame: you and me. Within the bubble, habitats teeter on the backs of multiple variables. Sometimes these threats stand alone. Other times they clump like cancer. They include everything from agricultural and urban dewatering of our lakes and rivers to rampant deforestation, river contamination, dams, encroaching invasive species, public vs. private-access flare-ups, and climate change question marks. The list goes on. In fact, they are all representative of the contemporary ills facing present-day Troutopia.

Brook trout in a box. A trout's underwater world is fragile and susceptible. How we choose to wade through the minefield of contemporary trout ills will dictate how their future unfolds.

In researching this book and talking trout with vested fisheries proponents, experts are fast to point out the absolute fragility and volatility contained within a trout's natural environment. This submerged world and its finned inhabitants are ultrasensitive to the minutest details from temperature fluctuations and spikes in pH to weather inconsistencies, low flow regimes, introduced competition, and the moments we step in and cast our flies. Nothing goes unnoticed.

Moreover, all components of a river, stream, or lake—alive, organic, and inanimate—serve specific purposes, and are mercilessly interconnected to trout health. Cool, oxygenated water and lush bankside vegetation ignite macroinvertebrate growth. Mayfly nymphs cling to prehistoric cobble. Caddis larvae live there, too. Migrating stoneflies shuffle toward reeds or a leaf of green grass to clumsily spread veined wings to a June breeze vaulting upstream along the Deschutes River. These and other fluttering morsels are indicative of thriving ecosystems and provide paint to the spotted canvas of cutthroat trout swimming Rocky Mountain National Park in spring. Bugs cling to the bellies of rocks; rocks crash downstream to the rhythm of run-off; trout hold against swift current—tails wagging, gills pulsating, filtering the ephemera. Thomas McGuane wisely wrote, "If the trout are lost, smash the state." And if the trout are lost, so too are the sinuous waterways that drive us to pursue chance encounters with life below their surfaces. Smash the bubble, and the stones and stoneflies and fishing stoners lose their collective roles. Smash it, and scratch fishing from our list of good things to do. Then, for whatever it's worth, go ahead and smash the state.

Indeed, how we choose to wade through the minefield of contemporary trout threats dictates whether Yellowstone River cutts can survive nonnative proliferation, how competing salmonids can coexist harmoniously in Washington's Olympic Peninsula, and whether or not diseased and dewatered rivers throughout the American West can rebound and reproduce life. The good news is that, in addition to being the problem, the solution also lies somewhere within the amassed brainpower of humankind. The wherewithal to find it is up to us and, in many cases, headway is being made.

Colorado's Arkansas River, for instance, is an example of a fishery that lost its bearings after years of neglect and abuse in the form of point-source pollution from mismanaged mines. In recent times conservation proponents have worked with water managers to pinpoint solutions that would fortify the system through four seasons. These improvements have come full circle over the past twenty years and the fishery and its trout have profited.

The Arkansas River clean up started taking shape in the early '90s, with a federally funded project engineered to stymie heavy-metal concentrations that seeped into the river during spring run-off. It was a massive undertaking that cost buckets of dollars and received little attention in the press. But fisheries proponents like Greg Felt, owner of fly shops in Salida and Buena Vista, noticed. Felt and his Arkansas River mainstay businesses have been fighting the good fight from the outset and helped see the project through to fruition. He says, "The river is a lot cleaner in terms of metals now and our fish, where they used to live to three or four years before they'd die from bioconcentrations of heavy metals, are now living to seven or eight years and seeing growth accordingly."

In addition to heavy-metal headaches, the Ark is a river where water quantity directly correlates to quality. Its flows have been historically choked at the neck and shipped off to parched yards in Colorado's Front Range, leaving a meager trickle behind to support its trout. In the upstream fishery near Salida, many of the Ark's major tributaries are managed for downstream water delivery. In the past, main stem brown and rainbow trout suffered when agricultural interests dipped their straws in, sucking the river near dry in summer and robbing the streambed of essential habitat. In recent times, river stewards such as Felt, together with the Colorado Division of Wildlife (CDOW), have made headway with local water managers to maintain trout healthy flows through hotter months.

"We've had real success connecting with those entities, both the feds at the Bureau of Reclamation and the southeast Colorado water conservancy district, which manages a significant amount of water in the drainage," Felt says. With that new water plan, the fishery and its trout are seeing success. Like Colorado's Poudre River and Montana's Madison, the Arkansas is another name on the long list of whirling disease victims in the Western US. But where Poudre biologists have struggled bumping rainbow populations back to their pre-whirling disease numbers, the Arkansas has thrived with the addition of Hofer-strain trout. These Hofer-Colorado River hybrids have a lower optimal water temperature range, and have made the river more productive more of the year. "It's changed the character of the fishery, broadened it and diversified it, and given us even more to work with," Felt says.

Today, the Arkansas stands as a premier blue-ribbon fishery. Its Mother's Day caddis hatch is legendary. Fly fishers flock there. And this reality is in large part thanks to thoughtful river proponents. Felt says support, as far as advocacy for the resource is concerned, continues to be strong: "I haven't really met anyone who hates rivers, clean water, or who hates trout. A lot of people, even if they don't fish, find it interesting and find it appealing. It's a positive association."

In addition to the Ark, positive associations that stem from wild trout in wild settings also remain prevalent on the North Platte River, where fisheries biologist Bill Wichers helped doctor Grey Reef flows to new trout-hospitable levels. Wichers took a river from the brink of collapse and turned it right-side up after Conoco spilled enough gasoline in a tributary to wipe out more than 100,000 trout upstream of the City of Casper. When replanted fish didn't take hold, Wichers stuck his head underwater to find out why. What he discovered was heavy siltation pouring in from upstream dams that sullied prime spawning habitat, cementing the cobble bottom and compromising the natural reproduction of the river's trout.

The flushing-flow regimes concocted by Wichers and Regional Fisheries Supervisor, Al Conder, were based on what they'd seen on healthy freestone rivers throughout the country. In the spring, snow melts and rivers rise, bearing the load of increased water. This prompts healthy adult rainbows and cutthroat to adopt their pre-spawn behavioral instincts. Ramped up flows scour the river bottom of fine sediments, and when trout move in to build redds and shoot milt, their prodigy are given a fighting chance in the cradle of cool, clean, oxygenated habitats.

Things like oil spills, siltation, and toxic mine tailings damage the riverscape from the top down. Wichers, Conder, and Felt—to a large degree—sourced fixes from the bottom up. When things are healthy under the water, our fishing opportunities above it grow exponentially . . . so long as they remain preserved in the public sphere.

. . . .

Across the border in Utah, another fisheries advocate who's made headway in the realm of trout habitat preservation, as well as fighting for public access to the rivers and streams we love to fish, is Steve Schmidt of Western Rivers Flyfisher. Schmidt began Western Rivers in Salt Lake City in the fall of 1986, alongside business partners Emmitt "Dean of the Green" Heath, and David Lattimore. During the past twenty-plus years he's witnessed the rise, fall, and rise again of fisheries such as the Provo, Weber, and Green Rivers. Schmidt's philosophy of what the sport should be and how he and his business advocate that is worth noting.

"As an industry, and in the name of capitalism, we've done great harm to this sport. We've put numbers on fish, sold them down the road, and in many respects stripped [fly fishing] of what made it special," he says. "It's the reason we aren't seeing any growth. Growth in my mind isn't a bad thing since we don't really have a lot a room to put more bodies on our waters. But it's ironic that the image the industry portrays isn't what it sells."

As a business operator who specializes in the commoditization of an unstable—at best—resource, Schmidt says he has a responsibility to be a steward of the fishing community, in addition to local environments: "From the products we sell to our efforts on our watersheds,

it's important to us that we participate and also get our customers involved."

One of the top threats to Utah fisheries in recent times, however, is less environmental and much more politically heated. And it revolves around public access to privately contested waters. In 2010 the Utah legislature passed HB 141: Recreational Use of Public Water on Private Property. This 2010 law changed a recreational easement recognized in an earlier Utah Supreme Court decision. In Conatser v. Johnson, the court ruled in favor of allowing the public to walk and fish on a privately owned streambed.

As it stands, new HB 141 legislation would stop recreational water users (including fly fishers, kayakers, tubers,

Business owner, Zen fly fisher, ardent conservationist, and all around good guy, Steve Schmidt (above, right), says we've spent too much time putting numbers on fish and selling them down the river. It's time to take responsibility for our resources today.

hunters, and others) from walking on the private bed of a public waterbody. So in a nutshell, if you're fishing in public water that flows over private property closed to trespass, you won't be walking on the land beneath the water without obtaining landowner permission. Without their blessing, you could see legal repercussions—all thanks to Utah legislators. In reaction to HB 141, the Utah Stream Access Coalition was formed and has since filed lawsuits challenging HB 141. Schmidt and Western Rivers have been on board since the beginning. The "good guys" recently won their first case. But the results will ultimately flow downstream, back to the decision-making machinery of the Utah Supreme Court.

Given threatened public access, coupled by the rarified resources trout fisheries have come to represent across the country, the preservationist crusade building against blockhead developers and yes-man politicians intent on stripping the public of its rights to fish, is gaining momentum. It's a mission that's tough to argue. Not only are there fewer places to fish, but in some instances there are just fewer salmonids left swimming in general. More fly fishers targeting them, too.

Peering inside Schmidt's mind, what becomes strikingly evident is a visionary ethos on how to approach the resource and how our time on it should be conducted—minus the constraints of commercialization. Fisheries biologist and Olympic Peninsula steelheader, John McMillan, shares similar sentiments. Before a recent trip to the OP, and weighing whether he wanted to fish with a scumbag journalist, McMillan forced two important points: 1) The current state of fly fishing pressure in the OP and helping prevent unneeded exposure to the already human-burdened fishery. And 2) he wanted to talk strike indicators. "I absolutely loathe the practice," he says.

As a fly fisher without any real Thingamabobber preferences or prejudices, I met request No. 1 with absolute agreement and No. 2 with a healthy dose of hesitation. Both Schmidt and McMillan have refused to fall under the indicator spell because of the added pressures it may (or may not) put on a fishery. Strike indicators can make catching trout and steelhead much easier, yes, and in that case a less-sporting pursuit, sure. If the ultimate goal of fly fishing is to embrace the challenge, in their view, the indicator is essentially a cheat. So I booked my tickets to Seattle, left all strike-indicator contraband at home, and the only wild buck I hooked and landed on that trip via Spey-rod remains one of the more rewarding catches of my life. So thank you, John.

Threats to fisheries come in many forms and for McMillan's beloved OP, these pristine rivers and their few remaining wild steelhead have been more worked over by poor fisheries management and ramped up angler traffic than anything else. When McMillan first moved to the OP in 1997, he had a few years of solitude and light fishing pressure. In the early 2000s the Washington Department of Fish & Wildlife closed Puget Sound streams early due to low returns of winter steelhead. OP fishing pressure ignited.

McMillan has been in the game long enough to recognize the dwindling resource wild steelhead have become and the need for a next generation of fly fishers to step up and draw swords for what's left before it's too late. He says: "I am not sure what the future of winter steelhead is on the OP. I believe there will be dramatic regulation changes in the next decade to reduce angling pressure because it is wholly unsustainable at this point. This is becoming increasingly palatable to people because the wildness of these rivers is being lost."

Imagine that—the *wildness* of a river being lost—and let it percolate. Like a car wreck stripping you of your ability to walk, our actions have impeded the ability of rivers to flow via nature's way and, in some cases, a trout's ability to swim freely. In instances such as favorite

Wild rivers home to wild fish make the underwater world go 'round. A small cutt with a big future in this coastal Washington tributary.

bottom-flow tailwaters, think Green or Missouri or South Platte, trout have benefitted along with fly fishers intent on chasing big bug events and bloated fish. Still in other cases, such as on the Yellowstone, preserving one of the country's first-rate freestone rivers—the longest undammed in the country—is a daily battle against non-native species integration and climate changes we can't turn back the clock on.

For now Yellowstone fisheries expert, Brad Shepard, has aimed his efforts toward underwater pockets still glimmering with a living, breathing currency in the form of native Yellowstone River cutthroat. He is generally optimistic about their future. "There are areas that are genetically isolated and in those areas we're fairly certain they will keep going," he says. "The problem is some of those areas are small and are at risk from fires, big floods, or drought that could wipe out 15 to 20 miles of stream."

The wiping out of 15 to 20 miles of stream may sound like smallish potatoes in the grand scheme of a robust trout fishery. But to put those numbers into perspective, 20 miles of Yellowstone equals about 3 percent of its entire drainage. If we were to eliminate 3 percent of the Earth's total land area—approximately 5,908,050 sq. miles—we're talking a swath larger than the continental US. The result would be catastrophic. And the effect on Yellowstone cutthroat populations would be the same.

Yvon Chouinard, of Patagonia Inc., told me, "We're living an unsustainable lifestyle on a very limited planet. You look at the history of the world and civilizations have come and gone. The ones that are gone have left us because they've exceeded their resources—every single one."

At the time, Chouinard was fishing May through November. His international itinerary included salmon, steelhead, and bonefish, and he had plans to fish Idaho, Wyoming, Yellowstone National Park, and British Columbia that summer. It was a solid lineup, and considering his not-so-rosy outlook for the planet, possibly a pre-apocalyptic one. Chouinard summed up that sentiment with some grim words on consumption and its effect on fish habitat moving forward: "Soon the money won't be in the banks anymore," he lamented. "It's going to be in the rivers. Unfortunately that's not too good for the fishing."

· ·

With mounting threats, good fishing remains for the moment. But the underwater bubble is in flux. From a trout's POV, rivers, stillwaters, and streams—from the Yellowstone to Henry's Lake to the North Fork of Nunyabidness Creek—provide all the creature comforts of home, minus flatscreen TVs and flush toilets. Trout get fat, rest and digest, migrate through a mix of varying habitats, and reproduce. But when their living quarters come under fire, survival takes a beating.

In their favor, trout have the ability to adapt. They've done an extraordinary job of this over the course of thousands of years on Earth. But the changes unfolding today are occurring so rapidly they're outpacing any chance for evolutionary Darwinisms. (Hence the hybrid phenomenon in stocked rivers such as the Poudre and Arkansas.) Warming water trends will force some trout to migrate to higher elevations and headwater habitats, if and when they have room to roam. Species such as browns will continue to thrive amid soupier-than-normal conditions. Warm water intolerants such as rainbows, cutts, and brookies might perish if it gets too hot. Other environmental factors simply eliminate the ifs and mights. Toxic chemical spills, siltation from deforestation, and dewatering to meet the demands of development offer trout little in the way of solace-seeking recourse. The effects are imminent. Mortality—even extirpation—the end result. But in certain places trout have been given a second lease on life thanks to some savvy maneuvering.

Over years of trials, errors, and successes, a formula has developed for what works—in contrast to the equations that have led us down the road to what doesn't. Healthy trout need ample and exceptional habitat. Underwater furnishings must provide respite from river temperature fluctuations. Suitable spawning grounds are a must, and a forage base brimming with aquatic invertebrates and underwater vegetation and riparian habitat is essential. Rivers that support these variables possess an underwater anatomy that mitigates seasonal spikes in flows, including the transport of heavy water and sediment loads during run-off. And, seemingly, the most coveted trout homes feature the internal elements that were chiseled into mountainsides that have weaved

The author exploring the critical junction of where the underwater world meets the one above. Healthy trout need ample and exceptional habitat. In the eleventh hour for many rivers across the nation, it's up to us to preserve and protect it.

through high-plains plateaus, stormed Triassic canyons, and meandered wide-open meadows, the way they were constructed by the hands of nature and time.

The fact that David Blauch and his team at Ecological Resource Consultants take backhoes to rivers to reinstate the building blocks for stream alignment, gradient, and equilibrium is a bizarre, unfortunate reality. But it's a reality nonetheless. Blauch tells us that a "manmade" or stream-enhanced section of river will never outperform nature's deliciously engineered course. And those words are a testament to where we've failed in the past and continue to fail today. Blauch says, "An undisturbed, natural environment is the best you're ever going to do.

When you get into a situation without influences from highways, railroads, mines, water diversions, and completely unnatural conditions. . . it's going to function the best."

But clearly now—in the eleventh hour for many rivers—nature needs a boost. Time cultivated underwater, crafting the pages for this story, has aimed to provide guidelines to becoming savvier, more learned fly fishers. Essentially, by "being the trout." These insights have also opened eyes to the vulnerabilities at hand. As fly fishers we take advantage of variables such as how trout feed and react to our flies. We've gained perspective on their underwater haunts, telling us what water characteristics lend best to understanding our quarry. We've strived to determine which flies, color combinations, riggings, and tackle preferences consistently bring the most fish to net. But we can't lose sight of the bottom line, which is maintaining habitat health to spark continued trout survival for perpetual human bewilderment. The business of fly fishing and catching must take a backseat to the preservation of species. Because without trout, simply smashing the state is not good enough.

The Steve Schmidts, Greg Felts, Yvon Chouinards, Brad Shepards, John McMillans, Roderick Haig-Browns, and so on and so forth—representing the enlightened factions of the fly-fishing community, past and present—get that. Trout, and their remarkable culture contained within the bubble, continue to benefit from the tireless work of river watchdogs across the nation. Meantime, the fishing is good. Let's get after it.

Index

Acknowledgments

This book would not have been possible without the family, friends, mentors, editors, and fishing crews who have endured enough obsessive behavior to drive lesser people to kick a man to the curb. Kat, Sam, and Mikey—you are my people (and dog). Thanks for sticking with me through a year of "Oscar Wildeing" it at the keyboard. (Here's hoping I don't die destitute in Paris at the age of forty-six.) Fred, Susan, and Dave Mueller. You are my family and I love you dearly. Your tireless support is appreciated beyond what these words can convey.

Stringing these pages together required a massive amount of time on the water and I'm grateful to those who fish—in particular with me. The North Platte River system is Stu Birdsong's cheese and crackers. Thanks for sharing your expansive knowledge, in addition to a couch in Casper and a seat in the drift boat. Big props to the Poudre River posse for springtime Picknick Rock floats. Fishing Colorado, Montana, Wyoming, and beyond has been nothing short of unreal with Tanner Irwin, Joel DeJong, Will Rice, Michael Gracie, Derek DeYoung, Don Yarbrough, Doug McKnight, Charles Craumer, Eric Ishiwata, Dave and Mike McCoy, Gifford Maythem, Bob Quigley, Kara Armano, John Sherman, Chris Santella, Oliver White, Adam Barker, Paul Weamer, John Barr, Vince Wilcox, Jin Choi, Frank Smethurst, Dave Katz, Aaron Alexander, and Grant and Julia Houx.

Thanks to the editorial staff at *Fly Fisherman* magazine: John Randolph and Ross Purnell for your guidance and taking a chance on a fledgling editor with a Canadian passport. Special thanks to Tom Bie for helping a writer land on two feet at the most fresh-thinking, fun, and irreverent magazine in fly fishing—*The Drake*. Kirk Deeter, you've been a solid wingman through many casts. Your belief in my words and adding this voice to a venerable list of writers at *Angling Trade* magazine is much appreciated. Dale West, your editorial ethos and commitment to story-first journalism are cornerstones we should all strive for.

Many of our wild trout and steelhead rivers are in a state of turmoil and change. The biologists, ecologists, river keepers, and stream stewards who maintain a keen eye on the systems (and fists in the fight) deserve high-fives. My gratitude goes out to those who helped make these pages turn from an underwater POV, including Brad Shepard, Fort Collins-based CDOW biologists, Ralph Cutter, David Blauch, Bill Wichers, Brian Chan, Greg Felt, John McMillan, and Steve Schmidt. Mr. Schmidt, you are a motivational force on the river. I hope the next generation takes the time to listen to what the stream has to say, and to follow in your well-worn boots.

There's perhaps no better place to start a life enveloped in fly fishing than the rivers and lakes of British Columbia. And I'm grateful to have spent many hours in pursuit of great fish with Rod Zavaduk, Peter Young, Paul Ratciffe, the West Kootenay Fly Club, Ron Thompson, and Brian Chan. Roderick Haig-Brown, your words on BC waters have been illuminating and continue to transcend space and time. Special thanks to Tim Romano for possessing the skills to pay the camera bills and your creative contributions to this project. Finally, I'd like to salute the Olympic Peninsula, the Rockies, Absarokas, Coasts, Catskills, Winds, Cascades, Bighorns, Selkirks, and Owl Creek Mountains for the waters and fish that course through you.

About the Author and Photographer

Geoff Mueller is senior editor at *The Drake* magazine and a contributing editor at *Angling Trade* magazine. He's fished in the Arctic, Argentina, Cuba, Mexico, the Bahamas, and more, and spends most of his on-the-water time chasing and studying trout in Colorado, Montana, and Wyoming.

Tim Romano is a frequent contributor to *Field & Stream* and a co-writer of the magazine's fly fishing blog, fsflytalk.com. He is the managing editor of *Angling Trade* magazine (the business publication for the fly fishing industry).